ALSO BY MORTIMER J. ADLER

*Dialectic*
*What Man Has Made of Man*
*How to Read a Book*
*A Dialectic of Morals*
*How to Think About War and Peace*
*The Revolution in Education* (with Milton Mayer)
*The Capitalist Manifesto* (with Louis O. Kelso)
*The Idea of Freedom* (2 vols.)
*The Conditions of Philosophy*
*The Difference of Man and the Difference It Makes*
*The Time of Our Lives*
*The Common Sense of Politics*
*The American Testament* (with William Gorman)
*Some Questions About Language*
*Philosopher at Large*
*Great Treasury of Western Thought* (edited with Charles Van Doren)
*Aristotle for Everybody*
*How to Think About God*
*Six Great Ideas*
*The Angels and Us*
*The Paideia Proposal*
*How to Speak / How to Listen*
*Paideia Problems and Possibilities*
*A Vision of the Future*
*The Paideia Program* (with Members of the Paideia Group)
*Ten Philosophical Mistakes*
*A Guidebook to Learning*
*We Hold These Truths*
*Reforming Education: The Opening of the American Mind* (edited
   by Geraldine Van Doren)
*Intellect: Mind Over Matter*
*Truth in Religion*
*Haves Without Have-Nots*
*Desires, Right & Wrong*
*A Second Look in the Rearview Mirror*
*The Great Ideas: A Lexicon of Western Thought*
*The Four Dimensions of Philosophy*
*Arts, the Arts, and the Great Ideas*

# Ten
# Philosophical
# Mistakes

## Mortimer J. Adler

A TOUCHSTONE BOOK
Published by Simon & Schuster

**TOUCHSTONE**
Rockefeller Center
1230 Avenue of the Americas
New York, New York 10020

TOUCHSTONE and colophon are registered trademarks
of Simon & Schuster Inc.

First Touchstone Edition 1996
First Collier Books Edition 1987

Manufactured in the United States of America

9   10   8

Library of Congress Cataloging-in-Publication Data
Adler, Mortimer Jerome, 1902–
Ten philosophical mistakes.
1. Philosophy   I. Title.
B72.A34     1987     100     86-29888
ISBN 0-684-81868-X

TO

*Wynn and Larry Aldrich*

# Contents

*To the Reader*                                                     xi

*Prologue: Little Errors in the Beginning*                         xiii

*The Ten Subjects About Which the Mistakes Are Made*                 1

## PART ONE

1. Consciousness and Its Objects                                     5

2. The Intellect and the Senses                                     30

3. Words and Meanings                                               54

4. Knowledge and Opinion                                            83

5. Moral Values                                                    108

## PART TWO

6. Happiness and Contentment                                      131

7. Freedom of Choice                                              145

[ ix ]

## Contents

8.  Human Nature                                   156

9.  Human Society                                  167

10. Human Existence                                178

*Epilogue: Modern Science and Ancient Wisdom*      191

# To the Reader

TITLES OF BOOKS are often misleading; sometimes they are inaccurate. Mine is not misleading, but it is inaccurate.

Readers will find that there are more than ten philosophical mistakes considered and corrected in this book. But there are ten subjects about which these mistakes are made. A completely accurate, but also more cumbersome, title would have been: *Ten Subjects About Which Philosophical Mistakes Have Been Made*. I trust readers will understand why I chose the shorter, though less accurate, title.

Readers will also find that the five chapters of Part One are longer than the five chapters of Part Two. The reason is that the mistakes discussed in Part One are more difficult to expound clearly. It is also more difficult to explain what is involved in correcting them. I should, perhaps, add that in my judgment the philosophical errors discussed in Part One are more fundamental and give rise to more serious consequences in modern thought.

## To the Reader

I have not tried to argue for or prove the truths that I have offered as corrections of the errors pointed out. I rely upon the reader's common sense to discern that the corrections have the ring of truth.

# Little Errors in the Beginning

### 1

"THE LEAST INITIAL deviation from the truth is multiplied later a thousandfold." So wrote Aristotle in the fourth century B.C.

Sixteen centuries later Thomas Aquinas echoed this observation. Paraphrasing it, he said in effect that little errors in the beginning lead to serious consequences in the end.

Neither Aristotle nor Aquinas had in mind the philosophical mistakes—all little errors in the beginning—with which this book is concerned. All of them are modern philosophical errors, mistakes made by philosophers since the seventeenth century, the century that was marked by departures in thought initiated by Thomas Hobbes in England and by René Descartes in France.

In one or two instances, the philosophical errors with

which we will be here concerned repeat errors that first occurred in antiquity. But this does not alter the fact that all
of these mistakes are typically, if not wholly, modern in
origin and in the serious consequences to which they have
led in modern thought.

Those serious consequences not only pervade contemporary philosophical thought, but also manifest themselves
in popular misconceptions widely prevalent today. They all
tend in the same direction. They affect our understanding
of ourselves, our lives, our institutions, and our experience. They mislead our action as well as becloud our
thought.

They are not cloistered errors of merely academic significance. They have been popularized and spread abroad in
a variety of ways. Many of us have unwittingly harbored
some of these mistakes in our minds without knowing
whence or how they came there.

## 2

To call these philosophical mistakes little errors is not to
belittle their importance. It is rather to say that they are
extremely simple mistakes, capable of being stated in a single
sentence or two. The truth that corrects them is corre-
spondingly simple and similarly capable of brief statement.

However, their simplicity does not preclude certain
complications. Some of these little errors involve a number
of related points. Some have a number of related aspects.
Some are dual mistakes, including both of two false extremes.

Seen in their simplicity, or even with their attendant
complications, they are mistakes that occur at the outset of
a long train of thought, leading from erroneous premises

through many steps to the false conclusions or consequences that those premises ultimately entail.

At the very beginning, before the consequences are discerned, the mistake appears innocent and goes unnoticed. Only when we are confronted with the repugnant conclusions to which cogent reasoning carries us are we impelled to retrace our steps to find out where we went wrong. Only then is the erroneous premise that at first appeared innocent revealed as the culprit—a wolf in sheep's clothing.

Unfortunately much of modern thought has not sought in this way to avoid conclusions that have been regarded as unacceptable for one reason or another. Instead of retracing the steps that lead back to their sources in little errors at the beginning, modern thinkers have tried in other ways to circumvent the result of the initial errors, often compounding the difficulties instead of overcoming them.

The advances that have been made in modern thought do not mitigate the disasters produced by conclusions that were not abandoned by discovering the initial mistakes from which they sprang. Making new starts by substituting true premises for false would have radically changed the picture that modern philosophy presents.

### 3

The order in which these philosophical mistakes are taken up in the following chapters is somewhat arbitrary, but not entirely so.

If their seriousness for human life and action had been the criterion for deciding which should come first, the order might have been reversed. The last six of the ten chapters concern matters that have more obvious practical importance for our everyday life. The first four seem more

theoretical, more remote from immediate interests.

However, though they are indeed more theoretical, the first four chapters deal with mistakes that underlie much of what follows. They are mistakes which have, among their serious consequences, little errors at the beginning of other lines of thought.

The mistake about consciousness with which the first chapter deals is, perhaps, the crucial one. It lies at the very foundation of modern thought. It determines its characteristic complexion. When combined with the mistake about the human mind that is treated in the second chapter, it sets modern thought off on a misadventure that includes many other turns in wrong directions.

### 4

The mistake dealt with in that first chapter may prove to be the most puzzling, even baffling, to readers because not only modern philosophers, but most other people are prone to making it. Without much reflection about it, they tend to suppose that they are directly aware of the contents of their own minds. They are, indeed, when they consciously feel pleasures and pains, or bodily strains and aches. Such feelings, however, are utterly different from their perceptions, memories, imaginations, dreams, and thoughts or concepts.

The latter let us call "ideas" for want of a single better word to cover them. Our ideas have the special characteristic and function of placing objects before our minds. It is always the idea's object of which we are directly conscious, not the idea itself. Ideas themselves are nothing but the means whereby we apprehend the objects they have the

power to place before our minds. They themselves are inapprehensible.

The second mistake compounds the error made by the first. The failure to distinguish between perceptual and conceptual thought—between perceiving the sensible objects that we encounter in everyday experience and thinking about objects that cannot be perceived or imagined—has serious consequences for our understanding of mathematics, theoretical physics, philosophy, and theology. It also has a direct bearing on the difference between the human mind and that of subhuman animals.

The third set of mistakes consists of errors that would not have been made in the philosophy of language—in attempts to explain the meaning of words—had it not been for the first two mistakes. The root of these errors lies in the failure to recognize that ideas *are* meanings. *As such,* they are the only source from which anything else—words and all other man-made signs and symbols—can acquire the meanings they have in our use of them.

The fourth mistake draws the line that divides knowledge from mere opinion in such a way that it puts mathematics, investigative science, and history on one side of that line and everything else on the other side. This amounts to denying the legitimacy of the claim made by philosophy to give us knowledge of reality and provide us with truths that are, perhaps, more fundamental and important than those we learn from science.

The fifth mistake also draws a line between what is genuine knowledge and mere opinion. This time it places all judgments about moral values—about what is good and evil, right and wrong, and all judgments about what ought and

ought not to be sought or done—on the side of mere opinion. There are no objectively valid and universally tenable moral standards or norms. This denial undermines the whole doctrine of natural, human rights, and, even worse, lends support to the dogmatic declaration that might makes right.

The sixth mistake follows hard upon the fifth. It consists in the identification of happiness—a word we all use for something that everyone seeks for its own sake—with the purely psychological state of contentment, which we experience when we have the satisfaction of getting what we want. Modern thought and people generally in our time have totally ignored the other meaning of happiness as the moral quality of a whole life well lived. This error together with two related errors—the failure to distinguish between needs and wants and between real and merely apparent goods—undermines all modern efforts to produce a sound moral philosophy.

The seventh mistake differs from all the rest. We are here concerned with the age-old controversy between those who affirm man's freedom of choice and determinists who deny it on scientific grounds. The failure here is one of understanding. This misunderstanding is accompanied, on the part of the determinists, by a mistaken view of the relation between free choice and moral responsibility. The issue between the two parties to the controversy is not joined. The determinists do not understand the grounds on which the case for free will and free choice rests. Hence their arguments miss the mark.

The eighth mistake consists in the astounding, yet in our day widely prevalent, denial of human nature. It goes to the extreme of asserting that nothing common to all human beings underlies the different behavioral tendencies and

characteristics we find in the subgroups of the human race.

The ninth mistake concerns the origin of various forms of human association—the family, the tribe or village, and the state or civil society. Failing to understand how the basic forms of human association are both natural and conventional (in this respect unlike the instinctively determined associations of other gregarious animals, which are natural only), it foists two totally unnecessary myths upon us—the myth of a primitive state of mankind in which individuals lived in total isolation from one another and the myth of the social contract by means of which they departed from that primitive state and entered into civil society.

The tenth mistake is a metaphysical one. It consists in an error that can be called the fallacy of reductionism—assigning a much greater reality to the parts of an organized whole than to the whole itself; or even worse, maintaining that only the ultimate component parts have reality and that the wholes they constitute are mere appearances, or even illusory. According to that view, the real existences that constitute the physical world are the elementary particles that are components of the atom. When we regard human individuals as having the real existence and the enduring identity that they *appear* to have, we are suffering an illusion. If that is the case, then again we are devoid of moral responsibility for our actions.

As I have pointed out, some of these mistakes have their prototypes in antiquity, but where that is the case we can find a refutation of them in Aristotle. The repetition of these mistakes in modern thought plainly indicates an ignorance of Aristotle's correction of them.

I hope that this brief summary of the ten subjects about which philosophical mistakes have been made in modern

times whets the reader's appetite for exploring them and for learning how they can be corrected or remedied. When readers have done that, they should turn to the Epilogue for a historical explanation of why these mistakes were made, who made them, and how they could have been avoided.

# The Ten Subjects
# About Which the
# Mistakes Are Made

# PART ONE

# CHAPTER 1
# Consciousness and Its Objects

## 1

LET US BEGIN with something everyone understands and ask some questions about it. It is to these questions that opposite answers are given—wrong answers and right ones.

When we are sleeping and not dreaming, we are unconscious. When we describe ourselves as unconscious, we are in effect saying that

— we are unaware of whatever is happening in the world around us or even in our own bodies,
— we are apprehending nothing; we are aware of nothing,
— our minds are blank or empty,
— we are experiencing nothing, or are living through an unexperienced interval of time.

To say that we are aware of nothing, or apprehending nothing, is equivalent to saying that we are perceiving

nothing, remembering nothing, imagining nothing, thinking of nothing. We might even add that we are sensing nothing and feeling nothing.

That set of words—perceiving, remembering, imagining, thinking, sensing, and feeling—comes very near to exhausting the acts in which our minds engage when we are awake and conscious. When none of these acts are occurring, our minds are blank and empty. When that is the case, it may also be said that we have no perceptions, memories, images, thoughts, sensations, or feelings.

At first blush, it would appear that much of the foregoing is repetitious. We seem to be saying the same thing over and over again. But that is not the case, as we shall soon see. Among the various statements made above, some lead to right and some to wrong answers to the pivotal question: When we are conscious, what is it that we are conscious of?

Let me put that question in other ways in which it can be asked. What are we aware of? What are we experiencing or having experiences of?

The crucial word in all these questions is the little preposition "of." Grammatically, it calls for an object. What is the object that provides the answer to all these related questions?

Still one more question: When we are conscious, and therefore our minds are not blank and empty, what are they filled with? It has become customary to speak of the stream of consciousness or the flow of thought to describe what successively fills our consciousness or makes up our experience from moment to moment. What does it consist of? In other words, what is the changing content of consciousness?

One answer to the question is given by using the word "idea" for all of the quite different sorts of things that fill our minds when we are conscious. That word has been so used by modern philosophers, notably by John Locke, who introduced the usage. In the Introduction to his *Essay Concerning Human Understanding*, he told his readers how he intended to use the word "idea," as follows:

Before I proceed on to what I have thought on this subject [human understanding], I must here in the entrance beg pardon of my reader for the frequent use of the word *idea*, which he will find in the following treatise. It being the term which, I think, serves best to stand for whatsoever is the *object* of the understanding when a man thinks, I have used it to express . . . *whatever it is which the mind can be employed about in thinking.* . . . I presume it will be easily granted me, that there are such ideas in men's minds: every one is conscious of them in himself; and men's words and actions will satisfy him that they are in others.

Locke's use of the word "thinking" is as omni-comprehensive as his use of the word "idea." He uses "thinking" for all the acts of the mind, just as he uses the word "idea" for all the objects of the mind when it is thinking, or for all the contents of consciousness when we are conscious.

Thus used, the word "thinking" stands for all the mental activities that, when distinguished, go by such names as "perceiving," "remembering," "imagining," "conceiving," "judging," "reasoning"; also "sensing" and "feeling." In the same way, the word "ideas," used in an omni-comprehensive fashion, covers a wide variety of items that can also be distinguished from one another: percepts, memories, images, thoughts or concepts, sensations, and feelings.

[7]

It would be unfair to Locke not to state at once that he does differentiate these various items, all of which he groups together under the one word "idea." He also distinguishes the different acts of the mind that bring ideas of all sorts into it, or that produce ideas for the mind to be conscious or aware of.

Let this be granted, but the question still remains whether Locke has distinguished them correctly or not. That in turn leads to the pivotal question with which we are here concerned: What are the objects of the mind when it is conscious of anything? The wrong answer to that question, with all the consequences that follow in its train, is the philosophical mistake with which this chapter deals.

2

In the introductory passage of Locke's *Essay* quoted above, two things are told to the reader.

One is that Locke expects him to agree that he has ideas in his own mind, ideas of which he is conscious.

The other is that the reader will concede that other individuals also have ideas in their own minds, ideas of which they, too, are conscious.

Since no one can be conscious of the ideas in the minds of others, Locke qualifies this second point by saying that, from the way others speak and behave, we infer that they, too, have ideas in their minds, often very like our own.

These two points together introduce a note of fundamental importance. The ideas in my mind are *my* ideas. The ideas in yours are *yours*. These possessive pronouns call attention to the fact that the ideas in anyone's mind are *subjective:* they belong to that one person and to no one else. Just as there are as many human minds in the world as there

are individual persons, so there are as many distinct sets of ideas as there are individually distinct minds.

Each person has his own. Only one's own ideas are, according to Locke, the objects of that person's awareness when he or she is conscious. No one can be conscious of another person's ideas. They are never objects of which anyone else is immediately aware. To concede that another individual also has ideas, of which we can have no direct awareness, must always result from an act of inference, based on what others say and do.

If the word "object" applied to ideas as that of which we are aware when we are conscious leads us to think that ideas are *objective* or have *objectivity*, then an apparent contradiction confronts us. We appear to be saying opposite things about ideas: on the one hand, that my ideas, being exclusively mine and not yours or anyone else's, are *subjective;* on the other hand, that my ideas also have *objectivity*.

We appear compelled to admit that, for any one individual, the ideas in the minds of other individuals are not objects of which he or she can be conscious. Their subjectivity puts them beyond the reach of his or her immediate awareness. In other words, the ideas in a given person's mind are objects for that person alone. They are beyond immediate apprehension for everyone else.

Let us pause for a moment to consider the meaning of the words "objective" and "subjective." We call something objective when it is the same for me, for you, and for anyone else. We call something subjective when it differs from one individual to another and when it is exclusively the possession of one individual and of no one else.

To reinforce this understanding of the distinction between the subjective and the objective, let me introduce

[9]

another pair of words: "public" and "private." These two words can be used to divide all our experience into that which is public and that which is private.

An experience is public if it is common to two or more individuals. It may not be actually common to all, but it must at least be potentially common to all. An experience is private if it belongs to one individual alone and cannot possibly be shared directly by anyone else.

Let me illustrate this division of all our experiences into public and private by proposing what I regard as (and what I hope readers will agree are) clear and indisputable examples of each type.

Our bodily feelings, including our emotions or passions, are private. My toothache, heartburn, or anger is something directly experienced by me alone. I can talk to you about it and if you, too, have had such bodily feelings, you can understand what I am talking about. But understanding what I am talking about is one thing; having these experiences yourself is quite another.

You may have had them in the past, and this may help you to understand what I am talking about. But you need not have them at the same time that I am having them in order to understand what I am talking about. In any case, you cannot ever share with me the bodily feelings that I am now having and talking to you about.

In sharp contrast to our bodily feelings, our perceptual experiences are public, not private. When you and I are sitting in the same room with a table between us on which there are glasses and a bottle of wine, you and I are perceptually apprehending the same objects—not our own ideas, but the table between us, the glasses, and the bottle of wine. If I move the table a little, or pour some wine from

the bottle into your glass, you and I are sharing the same experience. It is a public experience, as the taste of the wine or the heartburn it causes in me is not.

My perceptions (or percepts) are not identical with yours. Each of us has his own, as each of us has his own bodily feelings. But though my perceptions and yours are in this sense subjective (belonging exclusively to each of us alone), our having them results in our having a common or public experience, as the subjective bodily feelings we have do not.

To use Locke's terminology, both perceptions and bodily feelings are ideas and each of us has his own. But certain subjective ideas, such as bodily feelings, are exclusively subjective. They are objects of consciousness only for the one person who experiences them. Though they may be called objects for this reason, they do not have any objectivity. In contrast, other subjective ideas, such as percepts or perceptions, result in public, not private, experience, for their objects can be directly and simultaneously experienced by two or more individuals.

3

All ideas are subjective. I have mine; you have yours; and they are never identical or common to us both. They cannot be so, any more than the cells and tissues of your body can be identical or common with the cells and tissues of mine.

It is necessary here to introduce a distinction between ideas and bodily feelings, emotions, and sensations. Unfortunately, Locke fails to observe this distinction. Whatever can be properly called an idea has an object. Perceptions, memories, imaginations, and concepts or thoughts are ideas in this sense of the word, but bodily feelings, emotions,

and sensations are not. We apprehend them directly. They do not serve as the means whereby we apprehend anything else.

What I have just said applies also, in rare instances, to sensations generated by the stimulation of our external sense-organs, such as the sudden gleam of light we see, the unexpected loud noise we hear, the strange odor we cannot identify. These sensations do not enter into our perception of anything. In contrast, when we are perceiving, we are directly conscious of *something other* than our percepts.

What is that *something other?* The answer is: the table, wine bottle, and glasses that you and I perceive when we are sharing the experience that results from our perceptual activity. Our experience of the table, bottle, and glasses is a public experience, not a private experience exclusively our own.

These really existing things are the objects of our perceptual awareness, not the percepts or perceptions that enable us to be aware of or to apprehend them. That is why we can talk to one another about them as things we are experiencing in common. The table, for example, that is the perceptual object that we are both apprehending at the same time is the table that you and I can lift together and move to another part of the room.

For John Locke, the awareness we have of our own ideas is entirely a private experience, exclusively our own. This holds for all those who, in one way or another, adopt his view of ideas as the objects of our minds when we are conscious—objects of which we are immediately aware and that we directly apprehend. They are in effect saying that all the ideas that an individual has in his mind when he is conscious result in private experiences for him, experi-

ences no one else can share. To say this is the philosophical mistake that has such serious consequences in modern thought.

4

Before I point out the consequences of the philosophical mistake to be found in Locke's view of consciousness and its ideas, let me expound the opposite view a little further.

To state that view in its own terms will not only sharpen the issue created by the opposite views, it will also bring to light certain difficulties inherent in the opposing view. These need to be resolved.

Objections to the opposing view may already have occurred to readers of the foregoing pages. They may have noted the difficulties just referred to. They may think that the opposing view goes too far in the opposite direction and that it gives rise to consequences as objectionable as those resulting from Locke's view when that is carried to its logical conclusions.

It is necessary to remember that the opposing view does not apply to all ideas, but only to some. Excluded are bodily sensations, feelings, emotions, and, in rare instances, sensations generated by stimulation of our external sense-organs. All these are conceded to be private experiences, in which we are directly conscious of the pain we feel, the anger we suffer, or the sudden gleam of light, the unexpected loud noise, the strange odor that we cannot identify and that does not enter into our perception of anything.

All these are objects of immediate experience. They do not serve as means for apprehending anything else. They themselves are the objects of our apprehension.

With these exceptions noted, all our other ideas can be

[ 13 ]

characterized as cognitive—as instruments of cognition. Instead of being themselves objects of apprehension, they are the means by which we apprehend objects that are not ideas.

Those two little words "by which" hold the clue to the difference between Locke's view and the opposite view. For Locke, all ideas are *that which* we apprehend when we are conscious of anything. For the opposing view, some ideas (our cognitive ideas) are *that by which* we apprehend the objects of which we are conscious.

This view is expressed by Thomas Aquinas in a brief passage, comparable to the brief passage in Locke's Introduction to his *Essay Concerning Human Understanding*. I will paraphrase it in order to avoid terminology that might prove baffling to contemporary readers.

In the Treatise of Man, included in Part I of his *Summa Theologica*, Aquinas takes up the question whether our ideas (I am here using that term in Locke's omni-comprehensive sense) are *that which* we apprehend when we are conscious, or *that by which* we apprehend objects that are not ideas. With one qualification, to be reserved for later consideration when it becomes more appropriate, the answer he gives is emphatically: *that by which*.

Let me spell this answer out in all its significant details. It means that we experience perceived things, but never the percepts whereby we perceive them. We remember past events or happenings, but we are never aware of the memories by which we remember them. We can be aware of imagined or imaginary objects, but never the images by which we imagine them. We apprehend objects of thought, but never the concepts by which we think of them.

Do you mean to say (readers may ask) that I am never

conscious or aware of the memories or images I am able to call to mind, and that I cannot directly examine the concepts or conceptions my mind has been able to form?

The answer to that question, however contrary it may be to our loose habits of speech, is emphatically affirmative. A cognitive idea (including here percepts, memories, images, and concepts) cannot, at one and the same time, be both *that which* we directly apprehend and *that by which* we apprehend something else—some object that is not an idea in our own minds, but unlike our subjective ideas is rather something that can be an object of consideration or of conversation for two or more individuals.

Let us go back for a moment to the table at which you and I are sitting with its bottle of wine and its glasses. We noted earlier that our awareness of these objects was a public or communal experience, one that we both shared. It could not have been that if each of us was aware of nothing but his own perceptual ideas—his own sense perceptions. Its being a communal experience for both of us, one that we shared, depended on our both apprehending the same perceptual objects—the really existing table, bottle, and glasses—not our own quite private perceptions of them.

Subjective differences do enter into our perceptions of something that is one and the same common object for two or more people. They are usually not difficult to account for.

For example, you and I sitting at the same table and looking at the same bottle of wine report differences to one another. I say that the wine appears to have the color of burgundy, and you say that it appears to have the color of claret. After a moment's consideration, we realize that my perceiving it as having the darker shade of red is due to

the fact that I am sitting with my back to the light source and for me the bottle is in a shadow. You are sitting with light from the window falling directly on the bottle.

To take another example: you perceive the glasses on the table as tinted green, and I say that they look gray to me. You, then, ask me whether I am color-blind, and I confess that I forgot to mention that I was.

In spite of such subjective differences in perception, the object perceived remains the same individual thing for the different perceivers—the same bottle, the same glasses. The subjective differences, when noted, whether or not explained, would not cause the perceivers to doubt that they were looking at the same perceptual objects.

However, that might happen in the following instances. If I were to say of the bottle we are both looking at that it is half empty, and you were to say it is filled; or if I were to say it is corked, and you were to say it is uncorked; then we might have some doubts about our talking to one another about the same perceptual object. But it is difficult to imagine such perceptual differences occurring unless extraordinary and abnormal circumstances were at work.

Under ordinary conditions, perceptual experience is an apprehension of perceived objects. This applies also to memories, images, and conceptions. What is true of one type of cognitive idea, our perceptions, is true of all the other types of cognitive ideas—all of them the means, not the objects, of apprehension; *that by which*, not *that which*, we apprehend.

There is one important difference between our perceptions and our other cognitive ideas—our memories, images, and conceptions. In the case of the latter, our direct or immediate apprehension of the objects they put before

our minds leaves quite open the question whether these objects are or are not really existing things. Here are some examples of how that question arises

We remember some past event or happening. But we know that our memory can play tricks on us. We may, therefore, be cautious enough to ask whether what we remember really happened in the past as we are remembering it. There are various ways of finding this out. Having recourse to them, we satisfy ourselves that our memory was correct, and so we make the judgment that the event that is the object of our memory did really occur in the past as we remembered it.

It is necessary to note here that there are two separate acts of the mind. The first is an act of simple apprehension—the act whereby we remember a past event. The second is a more complex act of judgment, usually the result of reasoning or of weighing relevant evidence. The judgment may be either affirmative or negative. It may involve our asserting that what we remember did, in fact, really happen in the past, or it may consist in a denial that it did.

Turning from memory to imagination, we find that the question about the real existence of an imagined object arises in a different way. In most cases, the objects of our imagination are objects we construct from our perceptual experiences; for example, a centaur, a mermaid, or a mountain of gold. Because we have ourselves constructed them, we know at once that they are purely imaginary objects and so we do not hesitate for a moment to deny their real existence.

However, we are sometimes called upon to imagine something that can really exist and can be perceived, either by us or by someone else. Then we may, upon reflection,

affirm the real existence of the object we have imagined, but not perceived.

What is true of only some objects of imagination holds true for all objects of thought. For every object of thought that we apprehend by means of our concepts or conceptions, we face the question that calls for a judgment about its existence in reality. In addition to its being an object of thought, which may be a communal or public object that two or more persons can talk about with one another, is it also something that really exists? The object of thought, as we and others apprehend it and discuss it, remains the same whichever way this question is answered.

When, for example, angels are conceived as minds without bodies, they are objects of thought that can be discussed by two individuals, one of whom affirms their real existence and the other of whom denies it. While differing in their judgment on this point, they can still have the same object of thought before their minds and agree, in the light of the conception of angels they share, that angels do not occupy space in the same way that bodies do.

The question about the real existence of perceptual objects does not arise for most of our normal perceptions. Under normal circumstances, when we apprehend objects perceptually we, at the very same instant, make the judgment that asserts their real existence.

To say that I perceive the table at which you and I are sitting amounts to saying that it really exists. If I had the slightest doubt about its real existence, I would not dare to say that I perceive the table. In the case of normal perceptions, the simple act of apprehension is inseparable from the act of judgment that asserts the real existence of the object apprehended.

Hallucinations and dreams masquerade as perceptions. The person suffering a hallucination believes that he is perceiving what, in fact, he is not perceiving at all, because the object of his abnormal perception does not really exist. So, also, in the case of dreams: while we are dreaming, we suffer the illusion that we are having perceptual experiences.

The dreamer suffers an illusion of the same sort that the person hallucinating suffers. Both are taken in by the counterfeit perceptual experiences, and so they are deceived into believing at the time that these counterfeit perceptual objects really exist. Once awakened, or cured of hallucinosis, the illusion vanishes. Nothing in that experience was real; everything was imagined, not perceived.

## 5

The apprehended objects that are present to our minds through the agency of our cognitive ideas are public or communal objects. They are objects for two or more persons, objects that they can talk about with one another. This holds true for objects of thought and of memory and imagination, as well as for objects of perception.

It may be helpful to consider how a number of persons can be considering one and the same object when one of them is perceiving it, another is remembering it, and a third is imagining it. I shall postpone for later consideration (in the next chapter) how two or more persons can discuss the same object of thought. Since one of the three persons is perceiving the object common to all three by different modes of apprehension, we know that the object in question is one that really exists.

Let the physical thing in question be the wallpaper in a

woman's bedroom. The woman is sitting in her bedroom looking at the wallpaper while talking about it on the telephone to her husband. For her the wallpaper is a perceptual object; for him, it is a remembered object. Though the woman and her husband are operating with ideas that are not only numerically distinct but are also distinct in character (one a percept, the other a memory), the two ideas can present the same object to their minds.

Furthermore, if it is one and the same object that both are apprehending, though by different modes of apprehension, then it must also follow that the object being remembered by the husband must be an entity that also really exists, since that same object is an object being perceived by his wife. If that object were not an entity which also really existed, she could not be perceiving it. So far, then, we are able to say that the wallpaper has two modes of existence: real existence on the wall and objective existence as both something perceived and something remembered.

A little later the wife telephones a friend of hers and discusses the wallpaper, asking for advice about putting wallpaper of the identical pattern on the guest-room wall. The friend says that she has never seen the wallpaper in question. The wife then tells her friend that the pattern is the same as that of wallpaper on the friend's bedroom wall, except that the pattern is red on white, not blue on white. At this point the friend says that she can imagine the wallpaper and recommends putting it on the guest-room wall.

For the friend, the wallpaper is neither a perceived nor a remembered object. It is an imagined object. Though an image is different from a percept and a memory, it can nevertheless present the same object to the mind of the

friend that is present to the wife through perception and to the husband through memory.

It is thus one and the same object of discourse for all three of them. In addition, because it is an object of perception for one of them, that which is a common object for all three of them, though differently apprehended, must be an entity which also has physical existence on the bedroom wall. This is tantamount to saying that it is quite possible not only to remember but also to imagine an object that also really exists.

If two persons are talking about an object that is an object of memory for both of them, or an object of imagination for both, or an object of memory for one and an object of imagination for the other, the question about whether that common object is an entity which also really exists, which also once existed, or which also may exist in the future, cannot be so easily answered.

Let us consider first the case of two persons, both of whom are remembering the same object. That object may be an entity which now really exists and is, therefore, capable of being perceived by a third person. If that third person is not a party to the conversation, the conversation of the two persons about what at first appears to be a common object of memory requires them to exercise two cautions.

First, they must make a discursive effort to be sure that their numerically distinct memories have the same object. They can do this by asking each other questions about the object being remembered and thus become satisfied, with reasonable assurance, that it is the same object for both of them.

[ 21 ]

Second, they must not be precipitate in judging whether the remembered object either now really exists or once really existed and no longer does. Assuring themselves that they are both remembering the same object is hardly assurance that the object remembered is an entity that either has or had real existence. They could both be utterly deceived on this score, or be in some degree of error.

If they are not deceived or in error, and if the object that they are commonly remembering once had real existence but no longer really exists, can we say that one and the same entity has existence as an apprehended object and real existence as a thing?

The answer must be negative, since we know that the object being remembered no longer really exists. Nevertheless, it once did really exist. The fact that its two modes of existence are *not simultaneous*, as they are in the case of perception, does not alter the underlying principle.

What has just been said applies to the case of two persons, both of whom are imagining the same object. They must exercise the same cautions in order to be sure that the object each is imagining is common to them both; and in order to discuss the question whether that common object may also have real existence at some future time.

Such a discussion, for example, might take place about an invention that they are commonly imagining. If they concur in the judgment that the particular piece of apparatus they have used their imaginations to invent is an imagined object that is also capable of real existence in the future, the principle already stated applies; namely, that the object of their imaginations may at some future time also have real existence as a physical thing.

6

The opposing views of consciousness and its objects have now been sufficiently set forth for our present purposes. I have deferred the consideration of certain problems because they can be more appropriately dealt with in the next chapter, where we shall be concerned with opposing views about the human mind.

What remains for treatment here are the consequences of espousing one or the other of the opposing views. Let us first examine the consequences of the philosophical mistake. Then let us see if the view which corrects this mistake enables us to avoid consequences that we find repugnant to reason and to common sense.

Those who hold the mistaken view of ideas as *that which* each individual directly apprehends—the immediate objects of which each individual is conscious—lock each of us up in the private world of his or her own subjective experience.

It may be thought that, from the experience we have of our own ideas, we can somehow infer the existence of things that are not ideas in our minds—the existence of individuals other than ourselves, and of all the other bodies that, as a matter of common sense, we suppose to be constituents of the physical world.

However, since I can have no direct acquaintance with or immediate awareness of anything that is not an idea in my own mind, it is difficult to see how any attempt to argue for or prove the existence of an external reality can be carried out successfully.

The ultimate consequences to which we are thus led are so drastic and repugnant that the names we attach to them

are in general disrepute. No philosopher of sound mind has ever been willing to embrace or espouse them, even though, starting from Locke's little error in the beginning, Hume discovered that one is inexorably led to conclusions so extreme that common sense would prevent anyone from adopting them.

One of these extreme positions goes by the name of total skepticism concerning the possibility of our having any knowledge of a reality outside of or external to our own minds. The other is called solipsism—the assertion that everything of which I am aware or conscious is a figment of my own mind.

Common sense, in the light of experiences we all have, compels us to reject these conclusions as absurd. We cannot twist our minds into regarding all the conversations we have with other individuals as completely illusory—conversations in which you and I talk with one another about objects that we both experience, objects that we both refer to by the words we use to name them, among them objects that you and I can both handle at the same time that we are talking about them. We are certainly not talking about the ideas in my mind or the ideas in your mind.

Neither Locke nor any of his followers, including even the skeptical David Hume, lacked common sense. They had enough of it to prevent them from adopting the extreme conclusions to which the initial mistaken premise inexorably leads. In fact, Locke, in the opening passage in which he announces his use of the word "idea" to stand for whatever we are conscious of when we are awake, also announces that in the following pages of his *Essay* he is going to be concerned with the question whence come ideas into our minds.

Having, in Book I of the *Essay*, argued against the view that our minds at birth are endowed with innate ideas, Locke goes on in Book II to explain at length how our simplest ideas come into our minds by the action of external physical things on our bodily sense-organs. There is nothing in our minds that does not have its ultimate source in sense-experience. Locke's reiteration of this point reveals his tacit acknowledgment of the existence of Newton's world of bodies in motion, including our own and the bodies that act on us to stimulate our sense-organs.

One might think that rejecting as absurd the conclusions to which the initial mistaken premise inevitably leads would result in a rejection of the premise itself as equally absurd. That is the way a *reductio ad absurdum* argument is supposed to work. When we are shown that we have been led to an absurd conclusion by logically following out the implications of an initial premise, we are expected to respond by rejecting that premise as itself absurd.

That is what should have happened to Locke's initially mistaken premise. But it did not. On the contrary, the philosophical error with which we are here concerned was instead compounded by an effort to avoid its absurd consequences in another way, a way that did not involve rejecting the initial premise as itself absurd.

What was that other way? It consisted in saying that the ideas in our minds, at least some if not all of them, in addition to being the objects of which we are directly and immediately conscious, are also *representations* of things that really exist in the external, physical world. I have stressed the word that compounds the error.

When does one thing deserve to be called the representation of another? Only when we observe some resem-

blance between what is called a representation and the thing it is supposed to represent, as when we say that a portrait is a good likeness or representation of the person portrayed.

On this understanding of what a representation is, how can our ideas (the only objects with which we have direct acquaintance) be regarded as representations of really existing things (of which we cannot have any direct awareness at all)?

There is no satisfactory answer to this question. On the face of it, it is impossible to hold that ideas are the only objects that we do directly apprehend and yet are also representations of realities that are never objects that we directly apprehend, for one can be said to represent the other only if both can be directly apprehended and compared.

Nevertheless, illicitly converting ideas into representations somehow bolstered the ungrounded belief in an independent, external world of real existences, a world with which none of us, if imprisoned within the privacy of his or her own mind, could ever have conscious contact. The endorsement of this irrational belief is a mystery that has remained unsolved. The futile attempts to solve it have produced a variety of other mysteries, resulting in obscurities and perplexities that have riddled modern philosophy in the nineteenth and twentieth centuries.

Modern thought would have been better off if it had substituted the opposite view instead of engaging in all its serpentine twistings and turnings to extricate itself from the absurdities that result from regarding all ideas as the only objects directly apprehended. In addition, the foregoing mistake is compounded by the error of regarding

some ideas as representations of realities that cannot be directly apprehended.

The opposite view not only saves us easily from skepticism and solipsism; it also saves us from futile efforts to prove the existence of an external, physical reality.

In our perceptual experiences, we are directly acquainted with the existence of other bodies as well as our own. In addition, all the other objects about which we engage in conversation with one another—the events or happenings we remember, the fictions we can imagine, the objects of conceptual thought as well as the objects of our perceptual experience—all these are public, common, or communal objects that we can communicate with one another about.

We do not—in fact, we cannot—talk to one another about our own ideas—our percepts, our memories, our images, our thoughts or concepts. Our subjective feelings, yes; but not ideas that present objects to us. We are conscious only of the objects apprehended, not of the ideas by which we apprehend them.

The profound difference made by substituting the correct view for the mistaken one can be summed up as follows.

When ideas are treated as the only things with which we have direct acquaintance by our immediate awareness of them as objects apprehended, we are compelled to live in two worlds without any bridge between them.

One is the world of physical reality, in which our own bodies occupy space, move about, and interact with other bodies. Our belief in the existence of this world is a blind and irrational faith.

The other is the completely private world in which each of us is enclosed—the world in which our only experience is the experience constituted by consciousness of our own ideas. The assumption that individuals other than ourselves also and similarly live in the private worlds of their own conscious experience is as blind a faith as the belief that we all live together in the one world of external physical reality.

When we correct the initial error that generates all these results, we find ourselves living together in the world of physical reality, a world with which we have direct acquaintance in our perceptual experiences. We not only have bodily contact with one another in this world; we also communicate with one another about it when we discuss perceptual objects we can handle together.

That is not the only world in which we live together. We also live in the public world that is constituted by our common experience of objects other than the perceptual objects that are also perceptible physical things. I am here referring to past events or happenings that we remember, imaginary objects as well as things we imagine that may also exist or be capable of real existence, and all objects of thought.

There is still a third world in which we live—the world of our completely private, subjective experience, in which each of us is aware of his or her own bodily sensations, feelings, and emotions—experiences to which we alone are privy.

It would, perhaps, be more accurate and more consonant with common sense to speak of these three realms of experience as three dimensions of one and the same world, not as three separate worlds.

The three dimensions consist of (1) perceptual objects that are really existing things or events, (2) all other objects that may or may not exist, may have existed in the past but no longer exist, and objects that do not exist at present but may exist in the future, and (3) the subjective experiences that exist only for the individual mind that has them. The first two are public; the third, private. In addition, there are the cognitive ideas that have existence in the mind but, being the means whereby we apprehend all the objects we do apprehend, are themselves never apprehended.

Only when we fail to reject the fundamental mistake about consciousness and its ideas that was introduced by Locke, and perhaps by Descartes before him, is it appropriate to speak of the realm of physical reality, on the one hand, and the realm of the mind's conscious experience, on the other hand, as two separate worlds, the relation between which we cannot satisfactorily explain.

The philosophical mistake, when seen in all its consequences, is both repugnant to reason and to common sense. The correction of that mistake produces the opposite result—a coherent view of consciousness and its objects that involves no inexplicable beliefs and that accords with common sense and common experience.

# CHAPTER 2

# The Intellect and
# the Senses

## 1

ONCE AGAIN, let us begin with what all of us readily understand. We ordinarily speak of any living organism that has some consciousness of its environment and of itself as having a mind. We also attribute intelligence to that organism if, in addition to such consciousness, it reacts in some discriminating fashion to the environment of which it is aware.

It should be added, perhaps, that we generally regard mind and intelligence as the means by which sentient organisms learn from experience and modify their behavior accordingly.

By these criteria, the only animals to which we would not attribute mind or intelligence are those the behavior of which is completely determined by innate, preformed patterns of behavior that we call instincts.

[ 30 ]

The instinctive patterns of behavior of such insects as bees, ants, and termites are adequate for all the purposes of life and the survival of the species. Hence they do not need to learn from experience or modify their behavior in consequence of such learning. We are, therefore, justified in saying that they have no minds, no intelligence.

Among the vertebrates, and especially among the higher mammals, some behavior is instinctive in character, but not all. In fact, as we move up in the scale of animal life, the amount of behavior that is modified by learning increases in relation to the amount that remains purely instinctive and unmodified by experience.

By this criterion, we think we are warranted in saying that higher animals have minds and intelligence to a higher degree than lower animals. Of course, being sentient organisms, all have sense-organs; and it is through the functioning of their several senses that they learn from experience.

If we turn now from all infra-human organisms to man, a radical difference appears. In the strict sense of the term *instinct*, the human species has no instincts—no innate, preformed patterns of behavior. We have a small number of innate reflexes, only some of which are congenital. We also have what might be called instinctual drives or impulses. But in carrying these impulses out, members of the human species behave in a wide variety of ways. They do not all manifest a single pattern of behavior, such as we find in all members of a particular species of bee, ant, or termite.

In spite of this radical difference between the human and other animal species, it still remains appropriate to use such words as "mind" and "intelligence" in the same sense when

we apply them to humans and other animals. For us as well as for them, mind or intelligence stands for faculties or powers employed in learning from experience and in modifying behavior in consequence of such learning. Because we differ from other animals through being totally bereft of instincts, we need mind or intelligence to a higher degree. All of our adjustments to environment must be learned.

Much of the learning accomplished by the human mind or intelligence is based upon sense-experience. We have sense-organs that are generically the same as the sense-organs possessed by other species. The extent of the experience that their functioning provides us sets limits to our learning.

2

With all these quite obvious points noted, we are now prepared for the question to which right and wrong answers have been given in the twenty-five centuries of Western thought. The question concerns the human mind and its relation to the senses.

Is the human mind a single cognitive power, however complex, one that involves the functioning of our senses and whatever follows from their functioning, such as memory and imagination, *or* should the human mind be divided into two quite distinct cognitive powers—sense and everything to which sense gives rise, on the one hand, and intellect, able to understand, judge, and reason, on the other hand?

The question presents us with irreconcilable alternatives. One of these alternatives identifies the human mind with sense, including the whole range of consequences that

follow from our having sensations or sense-perceptions. The other alternative divides the human mind into two distinct parts—sense and intellect—and regards these two parts as performing quite different cognitive functions.

The first alternative constitutes the answer advanced in modern times, beginning with Thomas Hobbes and carried forward by his successors in British philosophy—by John Locke, George Berkeley, and David Hume, and by many others who came after them. It is, as I will try to show, the wrong answer—a mistake that has serious consequences.

The second alternative constitutes the answer that prevailed in antiquity and during the Middle Ages. It persisted in modern times, notably in the philosophy of René Descartes, Immanuel Kant, Georg Friedrich Hegel, and their followers. It is, in my judgment, the right answer, correcting the mistake and avoiding the consequences to which that mistake leads.

Among those who give the right answer, some go too far and their extremism needs correction. Before we come to that, let us consider the points that distinguish the right answer from the wrong one.

The first point, stressed again and again in the writings of Plato and Aristotle, is that the objects we apprehend divide into those that are sensible and those that are intelligible.

All of the objects we apprehend by sense-perception belong, of course, to the first group. That group also includes the sensible particulars we can remember and imagine—such as our memory of the dinner table at which we sat last evening, or our imagination of the house we are planning to build.

To the second group belong all purely intelligible objects, such as the objects of mathematical thought, or such metaphysical objects as purely spiritual beings; for example, souls, angels, and God. It also includes such objects of thought as liberty, justice, virtue, knowledge, the infinite, and even mind itself. None of these can ever be perceived by the senses. None is a sensible particular.

A second point follows immediately from the first. Since the objects we apprehend fall into these two distinct groups, we must have distinct powers of apprehending them—sense, on the one hand, and intellect, on the other.

It may be useful to repeat a third point, already mentioned. Sense includes a variety of powers, such as the power of perceiving, of remembering, and of imagining. Intellect also includes a variety of powers, such as the power of understanding, of judging, and of reasoning. We sometimes lump together all the results of exercising our sensitive powers under the head of *sense-experience*. So, too, we lump together all the operations of our intellectual powers under the head of *thought*.

Beyond these three points, shared by all those who give this answer to the question, certain divergencies must be noted. Plato and Descartes, and also later Kant and Hegel, go too far in their separation of the two realms—the sensible and the intelligible. This results from their attributing to the intellect an autonomy that makes its functioning, in some or all respects, independent of sense-experience.

This leads Plato and Descartes to endow the intellect with innate ideas—ideas it in no way derives from sense-experience. Kant's transcendental categories are another version of the same error. I have elsewhere, in a book entitled *The Angels and Us*, commented at length on this er-

ror, one that treats the human intellect as if it were an angel somehow encased in or associated with a human body.

The extremism just noted is avoided by acknowledging first, that the intellect depends for all its primary apprehensions upon sense-experience; and second, that, while some objects of thought are purely intelligible, our sense-experience provides us with objects that, with rare exceptions, are never purely sensible.

This second point needs a further word of explanation. The objects of our sense-experience are, for the most part, objects we not only perceive but also understand. Only when, in rare exceptional instances, we apprehend something as a unique individual that we are unable to classify in any way, is that object unintelligible.

Normally, the sensible objects we perceive, we perceive as particulars of one kind or another—a particular dog or cat, a particular hat or coat, a particular tree or flower. The particularized individual is an intelligible as well as a sensible object. We not only perceive it as this one individual thing. We also understand it to be a particular thing of a certain sort.

Sense and intellect have cooperated in our apprehension of it. It could not be a particular if it were not, at the same time, both a sensible and an intelligible object.

In contrast, such objects of thought as liberty, infinity, and God are purely intelligible objects. I will have more to say about their special character later.

Here I would like to add one further comment on the right answer to the question about the human mind and the senses. It enables us, retrospectively, to correct Locke's omni-comprehensive use of the word "idea."

In the preceding chapter, we focused entirely on Locke's

mistake in regarding ideas as always the objects of our understanding when we are conscious or are thinking about anything. We went along with his omni-comprehensive use of the word "idea" to cover sensations, perceptions, memories, images, feelings, and even what, in certain passages, he called abstract or general ideas. That all-purpose use of the word "idea" fitted in with his use of such other words as "mind" or "understanding" for a single cognitive faculty or power, essentially sensitive in character.

The opposite view that we have just been considering—the view that attributes two distinct cognitive powers or faculties to mankind, the sensitive and the intellectual—calls for changes in the use of all these words.

According to this view, our perceptions, memories, and images are *not* ideas. That word should be reserved exclusively for the concepts or conceptions by which we *either* apprehend purely intelligible objects of thought *or*, when our intellects cooperate with our sensitive powers, apprehend sensible particulars that are also intelligible.

Nor should "human understanding" be used, as Locke and Hume used it, for the human mind as a complex of sensitive powers. The English word "understanding" translates the Greek word *"nous"* and the Latin word *"intellectus."* It is paradoxical, to say the least, that it should have been adopted by Locke and Hume in expounding a view of the human mind that denies the presence of intellect as quite distinct from the senses.

When, in accordance with the opposite view, the word "ideas" is used exclusively for concepts or conceptions that are the instruments whereby we understand whatever is intelligible, we should remember that, according to this view, ideas or concepts are not that which we understand,

but only that by which we apprehend objects of thought, the objects we do understand.

In our everyday, loose speech, we frequently violate this critical caution. We speak or write about this idea or that as if it were the object under consideration. I am as guilty of such loose speech as everyone else. I have written books and given lectures about the great ideas. I have used the word "idea" in my titles as referring to an object of thought under consideration.

My only apology for this incorrect, loose usage of the word "idea" is that it would be both strange and cumbersome always to speak or write with the requisite precision. Instead of entitling a book *The Idea of Freedom,* I would have had to entitle it *Freedom as an Object of Thought.* Instead of lecturing or writing about the great ideas, I would have had to refer to the subjects of my discourse as great— basic or fundamental—objects of thought.

### 3

The mistaken view of mind, taken without qualification by Hobbes, Berkeley, and Hume, can be stated simply as follows: the mind, so far as it functions as a cognitive instrument, is entirely a sensitive faculty, without any trace of intellectuality about it.

All its "ideas" or "thoughts" (I have put these words within quotation marks to call attention to their misuse) are sensations, sense-perceptions, or images; and its images are either recalled sense-perceptions or they are constructed out of materials provided by sense-experience.

"Imagination," Hobbes writes, "is nothing but *decaying sense;* and is found in men and many other living creatures, as well sleeping as waking." In a subsequent pas-

sage, he tells us that "the imagination that is raised in man . . . by words, or other voluntary signs, is what we generally call *understanding*, and is common to man and beast."

Berkeley, similarly, divides all ideas into those of sense and those of imagination, distinguishing the former from the latter by their liveliness or vividness; and he, too, misuses the word "understanding" to name the cognitive power of the mind in sensing and imagining.

Likewise Hume, who in his *Enquiry Concerning Human Understanding* "divide[s] all the perceptions of the mind into two classes or species, which are distinguished by their different degrees of force or vivacity. The less forcible and lively are commonly denominated *Thoughts* or *Ideas*"; the more vivid Hume calls "impressions," by which he means "all our more lively perceptions, when we hear, or see, or feel."

In all these statements, two errors are compounded: one is the error of regarding our perceptions and images, miscalled "ideas," as the immediate objects of our consciousness; the other is the error of reducing the human mind to a purely sensitive faculty, able to be aware of nothing but what can be perceived through the senses or can be imagined as a result of our sense-perceptions.

I have omitted reference to Locke's *Essay Concerning Human Understanding* because, while that book commits the same two errors, it also contains passages in which the author takes notice of certain activities of the human mind that are intellectual rather than sensitive. A mind that was purely sensitive in character could not perform these activities. In spite of this, Locke does not explicitly acknowledge that the human mind consists of two distinct sets of

cognitive powers—those of sense, on the one hand, and those of the intellect, on the other hand.

All our "ideas," Locke declares, are not derived from sense. Some are derived from the mind's reflection about its own operations. It is aware of its own activities—its perceiving, its remembering, its imagining, and so on.

According to the opposing view of the human mind as constituted by intellect as well as by sense, it is only our intellectual power that is reflexive, not sense. The intellect has a self-awareness that the senses do not have. It is this fact that gives special significance to the distinction between ideas of sense and of reflection that Locke introduces, a distinction not to be found in Hobbes, Berkeley, and Hume.

The second qualification introduced by Locke is to be found in the passages in which he deals with what he calls "abstract or general ideas." Only man has such ideas; "brutes abstract not," he maintains.

Once again, it is the opposing view that gives special significance to this point in Locke; for, according to that view, abstraction is an activity of the intellect, not of sense. The human mind has abstract ideas (i.e., concepts) only because it is constituted not solely by sense, but by an intellect as well.

On this second point, the other three authors—Hobbes, Berkeley, and Hume—are most emphatically negative. They are more consistent than Locke in recognizing that, since the human mind is entirely a sensitive faculty, it cannot possibly have any abstract ideas.

Berkeley and Hume, who followed Locke and have read his *Essay*, explicitly attack him for his inconsistency on this

point. He should have realized that nothing abstract or general can be found in the whole range of sense-perceptions and imaginations.

Their criticism of him is well founded in a certain respect. Since Locke does not acknowledge the presence of a human intellect as quite distinct from all man's sensitive powers, his attempt to account for abstract, general ideas falters and fails. He affirms their existence, but he cannot explain them. He treats them as if they were like composite photographs, in which particularizing details are blurred by the superimposition of images upon images. That, as we shall see, is far removed from the abstract character of an intellectual concept, produced by an act of understanding that is radically different from any act of sense or imagination.

We now come to the crux of the issue between these opposite views of the human mind—one denying intellect, the other affirming it. It turns on opposite answers to one question: *Do we or do we not have abstract ideas (i.e., concepts) as well as sense-perceptions and images?*

Hobbes, Berkeley, and Hume flatly say that we do not. Locke fudges. He should have said we do not, but for a very good reason, which will appear presently, he could not bring himself to do so.

Of the three, Bishop Berkeley goes to the greatest length in his effort to expose what he regards as the utter nonsense of supposing that any idea can be abstract or general. A large part of the Introduction to his *Principles of Human Knowledge* is occupied with a refutation of this doctrine and with a critique of Locke for embracing it.

For brevity's sake, we can take Hume's summary of the

argument, to which he appends a footnote expressing his indebtedness to Berkeley.

Let any man try to conceive a triangle in general, which is neither *Isosceles* nor *Scalenum*, nor has any particular length or proportion of sides; and he will soon perceive the absurdity of all the scholastic notions with regard to abstraction and general ideas.

There we have it in a nutshell. If all we have are sense-perceptions and images derived from sense, then we can never be aware of anything but a particular triangle, one that is either isosceles, scalene, or equilateral, one that has a certain size or area, one the lines of which are either black or of some other color, and so on.

What is here said about triangles can be said in the same way of everything else. We are never aware of anything except particular individuals—whether by perception or by imagination—this cow or that, this tree or that, this chair or that, each with its own individuating characteristics, which make it this one particular instance of a certain kind of thing.

We may have a name for that certain kind, as we do when we use such words as "triangle," "cow," "tree," and "chair," but we have no idea of that kind as such. We have no idea or understanding of triangularity as such, or of what any individual must be like to be a particular triangle, cow, tree, or chair. Only our words (words such as the above that we call "common nouns") are general. Nothing in reality is general; everything there is particular. So, too, nothing in the mind is general; everything there is particular. Generality exists only in the words of our language, the words that are common, not proper, names.

Those who regard the human mind as having intellectual as well as sensitive powers have no difficulty whatsoever in meeting Hume's challenge head-on. By means of an abstract concept, we understand what is common to all the particular cows, trees, and chairs that we can perceive or imagine.

4

What serious consequences flow from the mistaken view of mind that denies intellect and, with it, concepts or abstract, general ideas?

The immediate consequence is an inherently untenable doctrine called nominalism. This is as repugnant to reason and common sense as the *isms* (subjectivism, solipsism, and complete skepticism) that, in the preceding chapter, we noted as consequences of the mistake about the objects of consciousness. A more remote consequence is one that affects our understanding of man's place in nature.

Before coming to that, I will try to explain why nominalism is inherently untenable. Showing that to be the case is tantamount to showing that the view of mind which inevitably leads to nominalism is also inherently untenable.

Locke's respect for reason and common sense prevented him from being a nominalist, even though his failure to acknowledge man's possession of a distinct intellectual power also prevented him from giving an adequate account of abstract, general ideas.

In Locke's view, the names we use derive their significance from the ideas in our minds to which they refer. Since our language includes names that have general significance, such as "triangle," "cow," "tree," and so on, we must have general ideas. Otherwise these names could have

no significance, for there would be nothing to which they could refer.

Correcting Locke's erroneous view of ideas as the objects of which we are directly conscious, we can restate his argument in the following manner. Unless, by means of our abstract concepts, we can understand triangularity as such or what is common to particular cows, trees, and chairs, the general or common names we use can have no significance, for they do not refer to this particular triangle or to that particular cow, but to triangles in general and cows in general.

How do nominalists who deny that anything general exists either in reality or in the human mind meet this argument and explain the significance of general names, the use of which they do concede?

They say that a common noun, such as "dog," is a general name, or a name that is general in its reference, because we apply it to any one of a number of particulars indifferently, i.e., without discriminating between this particular and that one in any way that would make the word "dog" inapplicable to both of them.

The general significance of the word "dog" is such, they hold, that I can use it today when I see a poodle coming down the lane and tomorrow when I see an Airedale coming down the lane, on both occasions being equally able to say "I see a dog coming down the lane." If, on both occasions, another person is present who hears my statement but is not looking in the same direction, he will understand that I am referring to a particular dog, but he will not know without looking whether I am referring to the same dog as yesterday or to a different dog. Either is possible.

The explanation offered, upon examination, reduces to the statement that a common or general name is one that can be applied to two or more individuals which are the same in a certain respect, or which have some characteristic or characteristics in common. To affirm this statement is, of course, tantamount to acknowledging that the two or more perceived objects to which a common name can be applied are particulars, each a unique or singular particular, but each a particular of a certain kind, to which the common or general name applies.

If all these particulars did not have something in common, or were not the same in certain respects, then one and the same common or general name could not be correctly applied to all of them *indifferently*, as those who take this view insist.

If, at this point, they were to deny that two or more things can be the same in any respect, or have anything in common, then the only explanation they have to offer would be undercut, and they would leave us with no explanation at all. Let us suppose, therefore, that they do not go to the extreme of denying that two things can have anything in common or be the same in any respect. We are, therefore, obliged to ask them whether we are able to apprehend what is common to two or more entities, or apprehend the respects in which they are the same.

If their answer to this question is negative, they have again completely undercut their own explanation of the meaning of common names as applicable to two or more items *indifferently* (i.e., with respect to some point in which they are *not different*). If we cannot apprehend any respect in which two or more items are the same, we cannot apply one and the same name to them indifferently.

The only alternative left open to them is an affirmative answer to the question: Are we able to apprehend what is common to two or more entities, or apprehend respects in which they are the same?

If they give that affirmative answer, because they must either give it or admit that they have no explanation to offer, then the giving of that answer is tantamount to a refutation of their original position.

To affirm that what is common to two or more things, or that what is the same about them, can be apprehended, is to posit an object of apprehension which is quite distinct from the object apprehended when we perceive this or that singular particular as such. But this is precisely the position which opponents of nominalism regard as the correct solution of the problem; namely, that there are objects of apprehension other than perceived particulars. Yet it is precisely this which is initially denied by those who deny intellect and, with it, all abstract concepts or general ideas.

5

Rejecting nominalism as a self-defeating doctrine, one need not go to the opposite extreme, the extreme to which Plato went.

Attributing to man an intellect independent of the senses, Plato also conferred an independent reality on its intelligible objects—the universal archetypes. In his view, it was these universal and eternal archetypes—of triangle and cow and everything else—that truly have being, and more reality than the ever-changing particulars of the sensible world.

It is not necessary to go to that extreme to correct the mistaken view of the human mind that regards it as a wholly sensitive faculty and that, denying intellect, is compelled

to adopt an untenable nominalism. To say that the objects of conceptual thought are always universals is not to assert that these universals exist *as such* in reality, independent of the human mind that apprehends them.

Suffice it to say that the intelligible universals of conceptual thought are public in the same way that the sensible particulars of perception, memory, and imagination are public. Just as two or more persons can talk to one another about a perceptual object or a remembered event that is commonly apprehended by them, so two or more persons can talk about liberty or justice as common objects of thought, or about triangularity and circularity, or about the difference between tree and shrub as distinct kinds of vegetation.

They can do so without any reference to the sensible particulars that may provide examples or instances of the universals they are discussing. It may be useful for them to refer to such particulars, when they are available, to make sure that they have the same object of thought before their minds; but there are other ways of identifying an object of thought to achieve such assurance.

A question still remains. Granted that the universals we apprehend as intelligible objects can be objects for two or more minds to consider and discuss, what about the reality of these universals?

In the case of perceptual objects, that question, as we have already observed, does not arise. What is perceived is a really existing individual thing; if it did not really exist, it could not be perceived. We would then be suffering counterfeits of perception; we would be hallucinating or dreaming.

In the case of the objects of memory or imagination, we

can ask whether the remembered object once existed in the past and, perhaps, whether it still exists; we can ask whether the imagined object may come into existence in the future. There are various ways of ascertaining the answers to such questions.

While the universal objects of thought never really exist *as such* (i.e., exist in reality independent of our minds), some measure of reality can be claimed for them.

We may be able to point to particular perceptual instances of them that really exist. We may remember particular instances of them that once existed in reality. We may even imagine particular instances of them that can have real existence in the future.

Whenever an intelligible universal can be instantiated (i.e., whenever we can point to perceived, remembered, or imagined particular instances of a conceptual object), we go beyond the object of thought to actual or possible real existences.

We need not do so. We can be content to deal with the object of thought *as such*, and go no further. Disregarding all actual or possible particular instances of the universal object we are thinking about, we may concentrate upon it for its own sake.

There is still one other way in which the universal objects of conceptual thought have a measure of reality. For a number of individuals to be particular instances of a certain universal, they must really have something in common. One example should help to make this point and its significance clear.

Let us take the universal object to which the common noun "swan" refers. This word names a kind that has instances in reality; it names a class of perceptible things that

has really existing members. To say that each of these instances is a particular swan is also to say that each participates in whatever is common to all swans.

Were there nothing common to all swans—nothing the same about them—the instances in question could not be apprehended as particular swans. To apprehend something as a particular instance of a certain kind involves an apprehension of the kind itself. That in turn depends upon the apprehension of what is common to or the same about the several instances being considered.

Hence, when in the case of the kind named by the word "swan" particular instances really exist, it is also true that the sameness that unites these really existing instances as particular swans is something that really exists in them. To deny such reality to a universal that has particular instances is as self-defeating as the nominalism which denies that we can apprehend universals, and then attributes generality only to words without being able to explain how words can have general significance if we are unable to apprehend any universal objects.

One further complication must be noted. Not all the universals that are the intelligible objects of conceptual thought are capable of instantiation by perceived, remembered, or imagined particulars. Instantiation (i.e., exemplification by particular instances) is possible only for those concepts that the intellect forms by abstraction from sense-experience.

Not all the concepts that the intellect is able to form are abstractions from sense-experience, as our concepts of cow, tree, and chair are. Some are intellectual constructions out of the conceptual materials that consist of concepts abstracted from sense.

In this respect, the intellect functions in a manner parallel to the imagination. Some of our images are memories of sense-perceptions, but some are constructs of the imagination—images constructed out of the materials of sense-experience; for example, the constructed image of a mermaid or a centaur.

We call these fictions of the imagination. So, too, conceptual constructs might be called fictions of the intellect, with this one very important difference. We acknowledge at once that the fictions of our imagination are objects that have no actual existence in reality. But many of the conceptual constructs that we employ in scientific and in philosophical thought concern objects such as black holes and quarks in physics, and God, spirits, and souls in metaphysics. These are objects about which it is of fundamental importance to ask about their existence in reality.

Since these conceptual constructs can have no perceptual instances, the attempt to answer this question must be indirect and inferential. The real existence of instances of such objects can be posited only on the grounds that, if they did not exist, then observed phenomena could not be adequately explained.

6

Charles Darwin's *Descent of Man*, published in 1871, more than a decade after his *Origin of Species*, rejected the traditional view of the status of the human species, a view that had been regnant in Western thought from antiquity down to the seventeenth century and, in some quarters, later than that.

According to the traditional view, man as a rational animal differs radically in kind from all other animals by vir-

tue of the fact that man and man alone has an intellect in addition to senses that humans share with other animals. Darwin marshaled evidence that attempted to show the opposite; namely, that man differed only in degree from other animals.

Hobbes and Hume anticipated Darwin by centuries, though this has often gone unnoticed. The most serious consequence of their mistaken view of the human mind as constituted by sense and imagination and devoid of intellect is the conclusion that men differ from other animals only in degree, not in kind.

They did not hesitate to draw that conclusion. For if the various powers that give us sense-experience and enable us to learn from it are common to the human and other animal species, then the only differences between humans and other animals must be differences in degree.

Since Darwin's day, experimentation with animals in psychological laboratories has turned up much additional evidence that has been regarded as reinforcing this conclusion. It has been interpreted as showing that other animals have concepts as well as percepts, even if they do not have intellects in the traditional sense of that term. Accompanying this attribution of conceptual intelligence to other animals has been the attribution to them of linguistic performances that are said to differ only in degree from the human use of language.

If these interpretations and attributions were correct, much of what has been said in the preceding pages would have to be withdrawn. but they are not correct. Reserving my criticism of the fallacious claims about the linguistic performances of other animals for the next chapter, I will concentrate here on the misinterpretation of the evidence

that is supposed to show that other animals have concepts that enable them to deal with generalities as well as with particulars.

To put the matter briefly, the experimental evidence does show that other animals, under laboratory conditions, can learn to discriminate between different kinds of perceived objects. They learn to react in one way to squares and in another way to circles, for example; or to eat what is placed on a green surface and to avoid what is placed on a red surface. Such discriminations indicate that they are able to generalize, and this is made the basis for attributing concepts as well as percepts to them.

The error here consists in thinking that to be able to discriminate between different kinds of objects is tantamount to being able to understand distinct kinds and their differences. To regard an animal's ability to discriminate between perceived similarities and dissimilarities as evidence of conceptual thought on the animal's part involves an equivocal use of the word "concept."

Strictly used, concepts are (a) acquired dispositions to recognize perceived objects as being of this kind or of that kind, and at the same time (b) to understand what this kind or that kind of object is like, and consequently (c) to perceive a number of perceived particulars as being the same in kind and to discriminate between them and other sensible particulars that are different in kind.

In addition, concepts are acquired dispositions to understand what certain kinds of objects are like both (a) when the objects, though perceptible, are not actually perceived, and (b) also when they are not perceptible at all, as is the case with all the conceptual constructs we employ in physics, mathematics, and metaphysics.

There is no empirical evidence whatsoever that concepts, thus precisely defined, are present in animal behavior. Their intelligence is entirely sensory. Its operations are limited to the world of perceptual objects and imaginable ones. What lies beyond perception and imagination is totally beyond the powers of the animal mind or intelligence. Only animals with intellects, only members of the human species, have the conceptual powers that enable them to deal with the unperceived, the imperceptible, and the unimaginable.

It is necessary to correct the mistaken view of the human mind first advanced by Hobbes, Berkeley, and Hume in order to defend the proposition that man differs radically in kind from all other animals.

The difference is one of kind rather than one of degree because only the human mind includes intellectual as well as sensitive powers. The difference in kind is radical because man's intellectual powers are not related to the action of the brain and nervous system in the same way that man's sensory powers are.

The full explanation of what has just been said is too elaborate for exposition here. I have dealt with it at length in two earlier books, *The Difference of Man and the Difference It Makes*, published in 1967, and *The Angels and Us*, published in 1982. However, one crucial point can be stated briefly here.

The relation of the sensory powers to the brain and nervous system is such that the degree to which an animal species possesses these powers depends on the size and complexity of its brain and nervous system. This is not the case with regard to the intellectual powers. That the human mind has such powers does not depend on the size or

complexity of the human brain. The action of the brain is only a necessary, but not the sufficient, condition for the functioning of the human mind and for the operations of conceptual thought. We do not think with our brains, even though we cannot think without them.

# CHAPTER 3
# Words and Meanings

1

EVERY ONE OF US has had the experience of looking at the pages of a foreign newspaper or of listening to a conversation being conducted in a foreign language. We realize that the printed marks on the page and the spoken sounds are words that have meaning for those who can read and speak the foreign language. But not for us. For us they are meaningless marks and sounds, and meaningless marks and sounds are no more words than are a baby's gurgles before the baby learns to make sounds that name things pointed at.

When a baby learns to speak and later to read, or when we learn a foreign language, marks and sounds (let us use the word "notations" to cover both) that were at first meaningless become meaningful. A meaningful notation is a word. Notations can be meaningless, but there are no meaningless words.

Another fact with which we are all acquainted is that most words have multiple meanings. One and the same word can have a wide variety of meanings. In addition, in the course of time, a word can lose one meaning and gain another—a new meaning.

A dictionary is the reference book we use when we wish to ascertain the various meanings of a particular word. The great dictionaries often give us the history of that word— the meanings it once had, but no longer; the new meanings it has recently acquired.

All of this is familiar to all of us. But we seldom stop to ask how that which at first was a meaningless notation acquired the meaning that turned it into a meaningful word— a unit in the vocabulary of a particular language, something to be found in the dictionary of that language. Where did the meaning or meanings acquired by that meaningless notation come from to turn it into a word?

Looking up the word in the dictionary does not answer that question. What you find when you look up a word is a set of other words that purport to state its meaning or meanings. If in that set of words there are one or two the meanings of which you do not know, you can, of course, look them up. What you will find again is another set of words that state their meanings, and either you will understand the meanings of all these words, or you will have to repeat the process of looking them up. If you knew the meanings of all the words in the dictionary, you would, of course, never resort to using it. But even if you did, the dictionary could not help you to find out how any one of the words it contains acquired meaning in the first place.

Let me be sure this is understood. Consider the person who refers to a dictionary to learn the meaning of the no-

tation that was at first glance a strange "word" or just a notation for him and so not yet a word at all. This procedure, while adequate for some notations, cannot be adequate for all. If the person's only approach to or means of learning a foreign language were a dictionary of that language, and one which used that language exclusively, he could not learn the meaning of any of its words. Only on the condition that he already knows or can somehow learn the meanings of a certain number of the words without the use of the dictionary, can the dictionary become useful as a way of learning the meanings of still other words in that language.

For a child to get to the point at which he can move effectively within the circle of a dictionary, some meaningless notations must have become meaningful words for him—*and became so without the help of a dictionary.* The dictionary, therefore, cannot be the answer to the question of how meaningless marks or sounds become meaningful words.

This is not to dismiss the usefulness of dictionaries. We often learn the meaning of a word that is new and strange by being told in other words that we do understand what that word means. Thus, for example, when a growing child hears the word "kindergarten" for the first time, and asks what it means, he may be quite satisfied with the answer "It is a place where children go to play with one another and to learn."

If the words in the answer are intelligible to the child, the child is able to add a new word to his vocabulary. A notation that was meaningless to him has become a word by means of a verbal description of the object signified. The answer to the child's question is like a dictionary defini-

tion—a verbal description of the object signified by the word in question. Such descriptions can be reinforced by what are called ostensive definitions—pointing to the object or word.

This, however, does not suffice as a solution to the problem of how meaningless notations become meaningful words for us. It holds for some words, but it cannot hold for all. We do learn the meaning of some words in our vocabularies by understanding the verbal descriptions of the objects they signify. But if we tried to apply that solution to all words, we would be going around in an endless circle that would defeat our search for a solution to the problem.

In what other way than by verbal descriptions can meaningless notations acquire meaning and become words? The answer is by direct acquaintance with the object that the meaningless notation is used to signify.

The simplest example of this is to be found in our learning the meaning of proper names. Whether or not we remember what we were taught in grammar school about the distinction between proper and common names, all of us know the difference between "George Washington" and "man" as names. The first names a unique, singular person—a one and only. The second names a distinct kind of living organism, a kind that includes only certain living organisms and excludes others. Words that name unique, singular objects are proper names; words that name kinds or classes of objects are common names.

I chose "George Washington" as an example of a proper name to make the point that we can learn the meaning of some proper names only by verbal descriptions. None of us has ever been or can be introduced to George Washington. We can have no direct acquaintance with him. We

know what his proper name means by being told that it signifies the first President of the United States.

The situation is quite different with other proper names—the names of all the persons in our own families or persons we have been introduced to in the course of our experience. The verbal introduction may be as brief as "Let me introduce you to John Smithers." But it accompanies your direct acquaintance with the object named. That is how "John Smithers" becomes for you the proper name of the person to whom you have been introduced.

So far, so good. But how do meaningless notations become significant *common*, as contrasted with *proper*, names by direct acquaintance rather than by means of verbal descriptions? Very much in the same way. The baby is told that the animal in his playroom is a dog or a doggie. This may be repeated a number of times. Soon the baby, pointing at the animal, utters "dog" or "doggie" or something that sounds like that. A significant common name has been added to the baby's vocabulary.

This will have to be confirmed by another step of learning. The baby may, on another occasion, find itself in the presence of another small animal, this time a cat, and call it a doggie. The error of designation must be corrected. Not all small animals are dogs. When the word "cat" has been added to the baby's vocabulary as a common name that signifies an object quite distinct from dog—both objects with which the baby has been directly acquainted—the two words not only have meaning for the child, but different meanings.

Have we solved the problem now? Not quite. For in the course of the child's growth, with his education in school

and college, and with all the learning that he acquires through a wide variety of experiences, his vocabulary of common names will be greatly expanded. Those same two objects that, in the nursery, he called cat and dog, he will be able to use other common names for, such as "feline" and "canine," "Persian" and "poodle," "mammal," "quadruped," "vertebrate," "domesticated animal," "pet," "living organism," and so on.

If we say that all of these common names acquired their significance through our direct acquaintance with the objects named, we should be sorely puzzled by the question of how the very same object of acquaintance can produce this extraordinary variety of results. If a meaningless notion gets meaning and becomes a word for us by being imposed on an object with which we are directly acquainted, how can one and the same object with which we are directly acquainted give quite distinct meanings to all the common names we use to refer to it?

The problem is further complicated by the fact that not all of the common names we use refer to objects that we perceive through our senses, such as cats and dogs. Not all signify perceptual objects with which we can have direct acquaintance.

What about such common names as "liberty," "equality," "justice," or "electron," "neutron," "positron," or "inflation," "credit," "tax shelter," or "mind," "spirit," "thought"? None of these is a perceptual object with which we can have direct acquaintance. How in these cases did what must have been at first meaningless notations get meaning and become useful words for us?

Is the answer that here all meanings were acquired by

verbal description? That answer we have already seen to be unsatisfactory because it sends us around in an endless circle.

Is the answer that here, too, we have direct acquaintance with the objects named, but acquaintance in other ways than through perception, memory, and imagination that ultimately rests on the use of our senses? If so, what is the nature of that direct acquaintance and what is the character of the objects named, with which we are acquainted by means other than the action of our senses leading to perception, imagination, and memory?

We are now confronted with a problem that modern philosophers have failed to solve because of a number of philosophical mistakes that they have made. Two of the three mistakes that I will report in this chapter and shall try to correct are consequences of the mistakes discussed in the two preceding chapters: one the mistake of treating our ideas—our perceptions, memories, imaginations, and conceptions or thoughts—as objects of which we are directly aware or conscious; the other the mistake of reducing all our cognitive powers to that of our senses and failing to distinguish between the senses and the intellect as quite distinct, though interdependent, ways of apprehending objects.

But before I turn to a consideration of the modern failure to solve the problem of how meaningless notations become words through acquiring meaning, I must call attention to one further point that should be familiar to all of us when we consider words and meanings.

A meaningful word, a notation with significance, is a sign. A sign functions by presenting to the mind for its attention an object other than itself. Thus, when I utter the word

"dog," you not only hear the word itself, but hearing the word serves to bring before your mind the object thus named.

Not all signs function in this way, especially signs that are not words. We say that clouds signify rain; that smoke signifies fire; that the ringing of the dinner bell signifies the meal is ready. Such signs, unlike words, are signals, whereas words are usually used not as signals, but as designators—signs that refer to the objects they name.

Words can, of course, function as signals as well as signs. "Fire" cried out in a crowded theatre not only designates the object thus named, but also signifies an imminent danger that calls for action. So, too, the word "dinner" shouted from the farmhouse steps to workers in the field functions exactly like the ringing of the dinner bell.

With one slight exception that need not concern us here, all signs are either signals or designators or both at different times when used with different intentions.

What is common to the signs we have so far considered, which are either signals or designators or both, is that they are themselves objects of which we are perceptually aware as well as instruments that function to bring to mind the objects they signify. Let us, then, call all such signals and designators instrumental signs. Their whole being does not consist in signifying. They have perceptible existence in themselves apart from signifying, but they are also instruments for functioning in that way.

The distinction between signs that are only and always signals and signs that are designators whether or not they are also signals will have a direct bearing, as we shall see, on one difference between the human use of signs and the use of signs by other animals. Another difference will turn

upon the one way in which animals acquire signs that are designators and the two ways that this happens in the case of human beings.

We will return to this matter in a later section of this chapter, but first, and most important, is the consideration of the problem we have posed about words in human vocabularies that function as signs that are designators. As we shall find, the solution of that problem will involve the discovery of another kind of designative sign, one the whole existence of which consists in signifying.

Like other signs, signs of this special kind present to the mind objects other than themselves. But unlike other signs, they themselves are entities of which we have no awareness whatsoever. They are thus radically distinct from the kind of signs we have called instrumental signs. Let us call them pure or formal signs.

The philosophical mistake to which we now turn consists in the neglect of pure or formal signs in the attempt to explain how meaningless notations get their designative significance and become words in the vocabularies of ordinary human languages.


2

In his *Essay Concerning Human Understanding* (1689), divided into four books, John Locke devotes the whole of the third book to words and their meanings. Having initially, in the very opening pages of the *Essay*, made the mistake of regarding ideas as the objects that we directly apprehend, or of which we are immediately conscious, he could not avoid a crucial mistake in his effort to explain how words get their meanings.

He was correct in thinking that meaningless notations

become meaningful words by our voluntarily imposing them on objects as the names of objects that we apprehend. This, as we have seen, holds for some words, but not for all—only for those the meaning of which for us depends upon our acquaintance with the object named, not for those the meaning of which for us depends upon verbal descriptions of the kind we find in dictionaries.

Locke neglected to observe this distinction between meanings acquired by direct acquaintance and meanings acquired by verbal description. Nevertheless, he was correct in thinking that our voluntary imposition of a meaningless notation upon an object apprehended is the way in which at least some words must acquire their meaning.

His mistake consisted in thinking that ideas are the objects to which *all* meaningful words directly refer and to nothing else. To say this is to say that when an individual uses words referentially, he is always and only referring to his own ideas and nothing else. "It is perverting the use of words," Locke wrote, "and brings unavoidable obscurity and confusion into their signification, whenever we make them [words] stand for anything but those ideas we have in our own minds."

Locke explicitly denied that individuals can use words to refer to the ideas in the minds of others. He even more firmly denied that individuals can use words to signify the things that exist in reality, their qualities or other attributes, or the events that occur in the world in which they live. We do not have and cannot have any direct awareness of such things. The only objects that we directly apprehend are our own ideas.

While being explicit and firm on these two points, Locke nevertheless realized that this account of how words get

meaning and have referential significance completely defeats the purpose that makes language so important in human life—communication. The ideas each individual has in his or her own mind exist in a domain that is completely private. How can two individuals talk to one another about their ideas, if the words each of them uses refer only to his or her own ideas? Even more perplexing is the fact that two individuals cannot talk to one another about the things or events that really exist or occur in the world in which they both live.

Having said that "words cannot be signs voluntarily imposed on things a man knows not," and having, throughout the *Essay*, maintained that we directly apprehend only our own ideas, not things existing in reality (which, according to Locke, act on our senses and cause us to have ideas), how can he explain our talking to one another about the real world that is constituted by "things a man knows not," i.e., things a man cannot directly apprehend?

The simple truth of the matter is that Locke cannot satisfactorily explain the use of language for the purpose of communication about the real world in which all of us live. The effort he makes to do so involves him in a contradiction as self-defeating as the embarrassment he cannot escape in positing the existence of the physical things that, acting on our senses, are the original causes of the ideas that arise in our minds; for, according to his own tenets, he has no way of apprehending such physical things and no basis for a belief in their existence.

Locke's efforts to explain what for him should be inexplicable involves a second step in his account of the significance of words. Our ideas being representations of the things that exist in reality, they themselves signify the

things they represent. Our ideas, in other words, are signs that refer to things, things we ourselves cannot directly apprehend. That being so (though there is no way of explaining how it is so), Locke's second step permits him to say that words, directly signifying our own ideas, indirectly refer to the real things that our ideas signify. Hence we can use words to talk to one another not about our own ideas, but about the real world in which we live.

3

If, as was argued in Chapter 1, the ideas in our minds are not *that which* we directly apprehend but rather *that by which* we apprehend whatever we do apprehend, all of Locke's contradictions and embarrassments can be avoided. The objects to which we give names and to which we refer when we use the words that signify them are the objects that we directly apprehend by our ideas, not the ideas by which we apprehend them. This, as we shall presently see, holds true just as much for the intelligible objects of conceptual thought as it does for the sensible objects of perception, memory, and imagination.

Earlier in this chapter, I called attention to the distinction between instrumental signs and formal signs. Instrumental signs—such as clouds signifying rain or the word "cloud" designating certain visible formations in the sky above—are themselves objects we apprehend as much as are the objects that these signs refer to. But a formal sign is never an object we apprehend. Its whole existence or being consists in the function it performs as a sign, referring to something we do apprehend, something it serves to bring before our minds. It is, as it were, self-effacing in its performance of this function.

The basic truth here, the one that corrects Locke's mistake and provides us with a satisfactory explanation of the meaning of words, is that the ideas in our minds are formal signs. Another way of saying this is that our ideas, as the signs of the objects they enable us to apprehend, *are* meanings.

Let me repeat this point: our ideas do not *have* meaning, they do not *acquire* meaning, they do *change, gain,* or *lose* meaning. Each of our ideas *is* a meaning and that is all it is. Mind is the realm in which meanings exist and through which everything else that has meaning acquires meaning.

The referential meanings that some of our words acquire when meaningless notations take on referential significance derive from their being voluntarily imposed on objects with which we have direct acquaintance. Those objects are the objects meant, signified, referred to, intended, brought before our minds, by the ideas that are their formal signs.

Locke would have us directly apprehend these formal signs (which are completely inapprehensible) and through them indirectly apprehend the things of reality (their representation of which is inexplicable). Accordingly, he mistakenly maintained that our words directly signify our ideas as their objects, and, through our ideas, indirectly signify the things of reality they represent.

The correction of this philosophical error consists in seeing that our ideas are the formal signs we can never apprehend. They enable us to apprehend all the objects we do apprehend. Those words that do not acquire meaning by verbal descriptions of the objects named acquire it by our direct acquaintance with objects that our ideas enable us to

apprehend. These are also the objects that our ideas, functioning as formal signs, refer to.

Furthermore, because the words we use have referential meaning as instrumental signs through association with the ideas that function as formal signs, we can use words not only to refer to the objects that we directly apprehend by means of our ideas, but also to arouse those associated ideas in the minds of others so that they have the same objects before their minds. It is in this way that we communicate with one another about objects that are public in the sense that they are objects apprehended by and so are common to two or more individuals.

This is of such great importance for us to understand that it deserves a more detailed exposition, first, with regard to the sensible objects we apprehend by perception, memory, or imagination; and second, with regard to the intelligible objects of conceptual thought. That exposition will be found in the next two sections.

4

The objects apprehended by perception differ in a radical way from the objects apprehended by our memory and our imagination.

The objects of our imagination may or may not exist in reality; they may be objects that do not now exist, yet may come into existence at some future time; they may even be purely fictional objects that do not exist, never have existed, and never will exist in reality.

The objects of our memory—past events that we claim to remember—may not have existed as we remember them.

Our memories can be challenged by others who claim to remember the event differently, or who even deny that what we claim to remember ever really occurred.

In other words, the objects of both our imagination and our memory are objects concerning which a question about their real existence can always be asked. That is not so in the case of perception.

When you or I say that we perceive the table at which we are both sitting, we are also asserting that that table exists in reality. If we are perceiving something, not having a hallucination (which is the very opposite of perceiving), then the object we are perceiving is also something that really exists.

We never should ask whether an object perceived really exists. The only possible question is whether we are in fact perceiving or are suffering a hallucination such as alcoholics suffer when they claim to see pink elephants that are not there.

Except for perceptual apprehension, apprehending an object does not involve the judgment that the object really exists as apprehended, or will exist in the future or did exist in the past. Apprehension and judgment are two distinct and separate acts of the mind, one first, the other second. Apprehensions as such are neither true nor false: they assert nothing. Only judgments make assertions—affirmations or denials—that are either true or false.

What is very special about perception is that, while here apprehension and judgment are distinct, they are also inseparable. To claim that we perceive something is to assert that the perceived object also really exists. If that judgment is false, then what we claim to be a perception is in fact a hallucination.

With these points in mind, we can now ask the question: Can one and the same object of discourse be a perceptual object for one person, a remembered object for another, and an imagined object for a third?* Since one of the three persons is referring to a perceptual object (in this case, let us assume that he is perceiving, not hallucinating), the object all three are talking about must also be something that really exists.

The case of a conversation between two persons about an object that one of them is remembering and the other imagining raises no new considerations. The same cautions must be exercised; the same principle applies.

Let us spend a moment more with regard to our using names to signify imaginary objects that are never objects of perception or memory. We often talk to one another about such objects. We are here concerned with objects that no one can perceive or remember because they are entities that never have existed in reality, do not now so exist, and never will. Let us call such objects "purely imaginary objects" or, as they are sometimes called, "fictions of the imagination."

Of all the creative arts, literature alone, because language is its medium, produces imaginary objects or fictions of the imagination about which we can communicate descriptively. The poet, novelist, or dramatist describes a fictional character which is the product of his imagination (Captain Ahab, for example, in *Moby Dick,* or for that matter the White Whale itself); or he describes some imaginary entity or place (the stately pleasure dome of

---

*This question is answered in detail in Chapter 1 and need not be repeated here. See pp. 19–22, *supra.*

Kublai Khan in Xanadu) which his imagination has produced. Depending on their powers of imagination, and the assiduity of their efforts, the readers of his work will be able to produce for themselves the same imaginary objects, or at least to achieve close approximations to them, sufficient for the purposes of conversation.

Such conversations take place in manifold forms and myriad instances whenever human beings talk to one another about books they have read. The fact that Captain Ahab or that the singular White Whale does not really exist, and never will exist, does not prevent persons from talking about these objects as common objects of reference, just as they talk about the incumbent President of the United States, or about Abraham Lincoln, or the white horse that George Washington rode, or the crossing of the Delaware at Valley Forge. If it were thought to be impossible for persons to converse about the imaginary objects initially produced by poets and writers of fiction, one would be forced to the contrafactual conclusion that a teacher of literature and his students could never engage in a discussion of a work that all of them have read. One need only think of the countless hours which have been devoted by students, teachers, literary critics, and others to the discussion of the character and actions of Shakespeare's Hamlet, to dismiss as preposterous even the faintest suggestion that imaginary objects cannot be common objects of discourse.

The mention of Shakespeare's Hamlet raises for us one final question about objects in the realm of the imaginary. Some of them, like the fictional characters of mythology (e.g., Cerberus or Charon), bear proper names that do not appear in the pages in history; but some, like Hamlet and

Julius Caesar, appear in Shakespeare's plays and also in writings that are usually not regarded as fictional.

The proper name "Hamlet" can be used to refer not only to the character created by Shakespeare, but also to what may be regarded as his prototype in the *Historiae Danicae* of Saxo Grammaticus, a twelfth-century Danish historian; in addition, if the account of Saxo Grammaticus is reliable, "Hamlet" was the proper name of a singular prince of Denmark, who lived at a certain time and was involved in regicide, usurpation, incest, and all the rest of it.

So, too, "Julius Caesar," as a proper name, refers to at least three different singular objects: (i) the leading character in a play by Shakespeare, (ii) a historical figure described in one of Plutarch's *Lives*, and (iii) the Roman general who lived at a certain time, who conquered Gaul, wrote a history of his battles in that province, crossed the Rubicon, and so on.

If we wish to talk about the character and actions of Julius Caesar as portrayed in the play of that title by Shakespeare, we must identify the imaginary object of our discourse by a definite description of it as "the character of that name in a play by Shakespeare, with the title *Julius Caesar*, first produced on such a date, etc." It would be confusion, indeed, if one of two persons who are engaged in a conversation about Julius Caesar used that proper name to refer to Shakespeare's Julius Caesar and the other used it to refer to Plutarch's Julius Caesar. They might get to the point of making contradictory statements about the apparently common object of their discourse, only to find that they did not have a common object, but were in fact talking about different objects—objects which resembled one another in certain respects, but which differed in others.

That Shakespeare's Julius Caesar is an imaginary object of discourse no one will question. The fact that there are certain resemblances between Shakespeare's Julius Caesar and Plutarch's and also between Plutarch's Julius Caesar and Rome's Julius Caesar, who was general, first consul, and dictator in the years 59–44 B.C., does not change the status of Shakespeare's invention. His Julius Caesar is a fiction of the imagination no less than Cerberus and Charon. Are we, by the force of this argument, led to the same conclusion about Plutarch's Julius Caesar and, therefore, about all of the historical personages described by historians and biographers?

## 5

Let us turn now from objects of perception, memory, and imagination, which are objects we name when we use words to refer to them, to objects of conceptual thought. We face at once the same problem that we faced before with regard to objects of memory and imagination. Here as there the apprehension of the object is not only distinct from, but also separate from, any judgment we may make about whether the object we are apprehending really exists.

To be more precise, the judgment should not be about whether the apprehended object of conceptual thought really exists, but rather whether one or more particular perceptible, or otherwise detectable, instances of it exist in reality. The reason for this is that the words which name the apprehended objects of conceptual thought are always common names. These are names that signify a kind or class of objects, not a unique singular object that is signified by a proper name.

The only way to ask about the existential reality of a kind

or class is to ask whether it is a null class (a class having no existent members at all) or a filled class (a class having one or more particular instances that really exist). In other words, kinds or classes, or what are sometimes called universals, do not really exist as such. All the constituents of reality are particular individuals. If the universals, or kinds or classes, have any reality at all, it lies in some property or attribute that is common to a number of particular instances that are all instances of the same kind or members of the same class.

What has just been said, by the way, explains how the perceptual object that the growing child names by calling it "doggie" can later be named by the educated adult using such words as "canine," "mammal," "quadruped," "vertebrate," "living organism." These other names signify one and the same perceptual object, but one that is conceptually understood in a variety of ways. As Aquinas pointed out, "we can give a name to an object only insofar as we understand it and according to the way we understand it." Since one and the same perceptual object can be conceptually understood in a variety of ways (i.e., can be understood as a particular instance of a variety of different kinds of classes), a whole set of common names can be used to refer to it.

With regard to many of the apprehended objects of conceptual thought that we use common names to signify, we seldom pause to ask the judgmental question about their real existence: Does one or more perceptible or detectable particular instances of the kind or class named really exist?

We would not think to ask it about white swans, but we certainly would if we happened to think about black swans. We would not ask it about dogs and cats, or trees and cows,

but we do ask it or have asked it about black holes, quarks, mesons, and other objects of contemporary theoretical physics, and also about angels, spirits, and other totally nonperceptible objects, yet objects we are able to think about by means of concepts that we form.

The foregoing account of the way we use words to name and refer to objects of conceptual thought brings us face to face once again with another serious philosophical mistake, widely prevalent in modern thought, though not exclusively modern in origin.

It is the error known as nominalism. It consists in the denial of what are sometimes called "abstract ideas," sometimes "general concepts," but which, however named, are ideas that enable us to understand kinds or classes without any reference to particular perceptual instances that may or may not exist.

These are the ideas through the functioning of which the common names in our vocabulary signify and refer to the kinds or classes that they enable us to apprehend as objects of thought. The nominalist's denial that we have such ideas compels him to try to offer another explanation of the meaning or significance of common names or what are sometimes called general terms. I have shown that all his efforts to do so are self-defeating.*

6

Another mistake about language that follows as a consequence of the failure to distinguish the human intellect from the senses is, strictly speaking, not a philosophical mistake. It is one of which animal psychologists and behav-

---

*See Section 4 of Chapter 2, *supra*.

ioral scientists are for the most part guilty, though many contemporary philosophers associate themselves with the position taken by students of animal behavior.

In their study of the evidence of animal communication, they seldom if ever note the difference between signs that function merely as signals and signs that function as designators—as names that refer to objects. Almost all of the cries, sounds, gestures, that animals in the wild, and domesticated animals as well, use to express their emotions and desires, serve as signals, not as designators. It is only in the laboratory and under experimental conditions, often with very ingeniously contrived special apparatus, that such higher mammals as chimpanzees and bottle-nosed dolphins *appear* to be communicating by using words *as if* they were names, and even to be making sentences by putting them together with some vestige of syntax.

The appearance is then misinterpreted by the scientists as a basis for asserting that the only difference between animal and human language is one of degree, not of kind—a difference in the number of name words in an animal's vocabulary and a difference in the complexity of the utterances that are taken to be sentences.

This misinterpretation arises from the neglect or ignorance, on the part of the scientists, of the difference between perceptual and conceptual thought. That, in turn, stems from their failure to acknowledge the difference between the senses and the intellect or their denial that the difference exists.

That these differences should not be ignored and cannot be denied would have to be conceded by anyone who looked at the evidence with an unprejudiced eye—by anyone who did not start out with the firm intention of showing that

humans and brutes differ only in degree. While there is evidence that chimpanzees under experimental conditions do use artificially contrived signs to designate or name things, the things they name are all perceptual objects. There is not a single piece of evidence showing their ability to use signs to designate what is not perceived through their senses or what lies totally beyond the sensible realm and is intrinsically imperceptible.

Therein lies the difference between the animal's power of perceptual thought and the human power of conceptual thought. There is no doubt that the animal's power of perceptual thought enables it to perform acts of abstraction and generalization that have a certain similitude to human abstraction and generalization.

The animal's behavior manifests different reactions to objects that are different in kind. But the kinds of things that animals appear to differentiate are all kinds of which there are perceptual instances in the animal's experience. Humans differentiate kinds or classes of which there either are no perceptual instances in their experience or of which there cannot be any. This is the distinguishing characteristic of conceptual thought and the irrefutable evidence of the presence of intellect in man and of its absence in brutes.

One further observation, if it were made by the animal psychologists, might open their eyes to the difference in kind, not degree, between human language and the acquirement by animals of signs that appear to function as designative names. It involves the distinction, already made, between a word acquiring its designative meaning through direct perceptual acquaintance with the object named and the acquirement of meaning by means of a verbal description, as when a child learns the meaning of the word "kin-

dergarten" by being told that it is a place where children get together to play and learn.

In all the experimental work done on animals, there is no instance where a sign that an animal uses gets its meaning from a collocation of other signs that purport to express its meaning. In every case, a new sign that is introduced into the animal's vocabulary becomes meaningful through being attached to a perceptual object with which the animal has direct acquaintance.

If the students of animal behavior had engaged in their observations and experiments with a recognition of the difference between perceptual and conceptual thought, and with an acknowledgment that humans have intellect as well as senses, whereas animals lack intellects, they would not be so prone to ignore or deny the difference in kind between the human and animal use of signs as names or designators.

7

Finally, we come to one more philosophical mistake that has had very serious consequences for the contemporary philosophy of language. Unlike all the errors noted in the preceding sections of this chapter, it is not a mistake that stems from errors discussed in Chapters 1 and 2.

This mistake is introduced into modern thought by Thomas Hobbes in his *Leviathan* (1651), Chapter 4 of which is concerned with speech. In the centuries before Hobbes, the term *meaningless* had a purely descriptive significance. It signified that a sound or mark simply lacked meaning; that it was like the nonsense syllables "glub" and "trish."

Hobbes introduced a dyslogistic use of the term *meaningless*. For him a word like "angel" or its equivalent phrase

"incorporeal substance" is a meaningless expression because of his espousal of materialism as a metaphysical doctrine, according to which only bodies or material things exist in reality. Since angels or incorporeal substances according to this doctrine do not exist, the words "angel" or "incorporeal substance" must be meaningless. They designate nothing; they refer to nothing.

Hobbes compounds the error he is here making by maintaining that such an expression as "incorporeal substance" is a contradiction in terms and cannot exist. Even if one were to grant him the truth of his materialistic premise that nothing exists except bodies or corporeal substances, it would still not cogently follow that incorporeal substances, or angels, *cannot possibly exist*. The only conclusion to be drawn from that premise is that angels do not exist, not that they are impossible, because self-contradictory in the same way that the phrase "round square" is self-contradictory.

That, however, is not the main point to be considered. The main point is that Hobbes reduced the designative reference of name words to the one mode of reference which involves a reference to some really existent thing or to a class of things of which there are really existent instances.

If we merely ask the question whether angels do or do not exist, and certainly if we affirm or deny that they do, the word "angel" must have some meaning. If it were totally meaningless, as Hobbes declares, we could not ask the question, or make the affirmation or denial, any more than we could ask whether glub exists or deny that trish does.

The only truly meaningless notations are either nonsense syllables, such as "glub" and "trish," or a contradiction in terms, such as "round square." A round square is

simply inconceivable or unthinkable. That being so, there can be no idea of it, and no object of thought which we can apprehend. Hence the phrase designates or refers to nothing.

"If a man should speak to me about *immaterial substances*, or about a *free subject*, a *free will*," Hobbes writes, "I should not say he were in error, but that his words were without meaning; that is to say, absurd." He goes on to say that statements about things that never have been, "nor can be incident to sense," are absurd speeches, "taken upon credit, *without any signification at all*."

The focal point of Hobbes' error is the elimination of all designative references that are not also existentially denotative (i.e., references to the really existent). As we observed earlier, except for special proper names and the common names for objects perceived, not hallucinated, all other common names have designative references that are *not* also existentially denotative. About almost all the objects of memory and imagination that we can name, certainly about all the objects of conceptual thought that we can name, the question whether what is named has existence in reality should be asked.

If such objects, about which that question should be asked, cannot be named by signs that have referential significance, then questions that should be asked simply cannot be asked. The elimination of referential significance that is not also existentially denotative would make it impossible to ask such questions.

The twentieth-century followers of Hobbes, even those who do know that they are elaborating extensively on a point that he mentioned briefly and then dismissed as not worthy of further comment, try to avoid the impossibility just

mentioned by distinguishing between what they call "sense" and "reference."

For them, the only referential significance that name words can have involves existential denotation—reference to the really existent. A relatively small number of special proper names, or their equivalents in phrases that are definite descriptions, such as "the first President of the United States," have such referential significance.

All the rest of the words in our vocabulary have only sense, but not reference. That sense consists in their connotation, which can be expressed in a set of other words. But they refer to nothing at all.

How do these modern linguistic philosophers reach such an absurd conclusion? What is its root or origin? The only explanation, in my judgment, is that it lies in their ignorance of the distinction between formal and instrumental signs and in their consequent failure to understand that the words which become names through direct acquaintance with the objects named refer to whatever objects are signified by the ideas in our mind functioning as formal signs of those objects.

Accordingly, all the words that name the objects of thought, about which we should ask the existential question, do have referential significance. Their designative meaning consists in their reference to such objects, whether or not any instances of them can be perceived because they actually exist in reality. Such words have more than sense, or merely connotative meaning. They have as much referential significance as any correctly used proper name or definite description.

This reductionist error, which consists in reducing referential significance to the one mode of significance that

involves a reference to something really existent, lies at the heart of Bertrand Russell's famous theory of descriptions. And what lies at the heart of that error is the mistake of supposing that naming is asserting—that we cannot name something without also asserting that the thing named really exists.

Naming is not asserting, any more than apprehending an object of thought is identical with making the judgment that the object has existence in reality. Apprehending an object and making the judgment that it really exists are insepa- rable only in the case of veridical perceptions. In every other case, the acts of apprehension and judgment are not only distinct but also quite separate. One act can occur without the other occurring. Hence we can use words to refer to apprehended objects about the existence of which we sus- pend judgment or ask questions.

As a result of these errors, originating with Hobbes, lin- guistic philosophy in the twentieth century has abandoned the effort to explain the referential significance of most words in our daily vocabulary—all words that do not have the one mode of referential significance that denotes something really existent (according to whatever metaphysical doctrine may be held about the components of reality).

This has led to the fatuous injunction "Don't look for the meaning; look for the use," as if it were possible to discover the use of a word without first ascertaining its meaning as used, a meaning that it must have had before it was used in order to be used in one certain way rather than another. Language does not control thought, as con- temporary linguistic philosophers appear to believe. It is the other way around.

Another possible explanation of the abandonment by

contemporary linguistic philosophers of any attempt to account for the lexical meanings of most of the words in our daily vocabularies is their awareness of the embarrassments that Locke's attempt to do so could not avoid. Unable to avoid the mistakes made by Locke and unable to give a correct account of the matter because they were ignorant of the insights and distinctions required to do so, they gave the whole thing up as a bad job.

# CHAPTER 4
# Knowledge and Opinion

## 1

ALL MEN, ARISTOTLE SAID, by nature desire to know. It may not be true that, born with that native propensity, all persons in fact continue to nourish it. But certainly there are but few who do not regard knowledge as desirable, as a good to be prized, and a good without limit—the more, the better.

It is generally understood that those who have knowledge about anything are in the possession of the truth about it. Individuals may at times be incorrect in their claim that they do have knowledge, but if they do, then they have some hold on the truth. The phrase "false knowledge" is a contradiction in terms; "true knowledge" is manifestly redundant.

That being understood, the line that divides knowledge from opinion should also be clear. There is nothing self-

contradictory in the phrase "true opinion," or redundant in the phrase "false opinion." Opinions can be true or false, as knowledge cannot be. When individuals claim to have knowledge about something that turns out not to be knowledge at all because it is false, what they mistook for knowledge was only opinion.

Closely connected with this distinction between knowledge and opinion are two other distinctions. One is the distinction between the things about which we can have certitude—beyond any shadow of a doubt—and things about which some doubt remains. We may be persuaded by them beyond a reasonable doubt, but that does not take them entirely out of the realm of doubt. Some doubt lingers.

The other distinction is that between the corrigible and mutable and the incorrigible and immutable. When we have certitude about anything, we have a hold on truth that is both incorrigible and immutable. When anything remains in doubt, to even the slightest degree, it is both mutable and corrigible. We should recognize that we may change our minds about it and correct whatever was wrong.

By these criteria for distinguishing between knowledge and opinion, how much knowledge do any of us have? Most of us would admit that we have precious little. Most of us are aware that in the history of science even the most revered formulations have been subject to change and correction. Yet at the same time most of us would be reluctant to say that the great generalizations or conclusions of science, those now regnant, are nothing but mere opinions. The word "opinion," especially when it is qualified by the word "mere," carries such a derogatory connotation that we feel, quite properly, that to call science opinion rather than knowledge is inadmissible.

The only way out of this difficulty that I know is one that I proposed in an earlier book that contained a series of chapters on the idea of truth.* I repeat it here in order to lay the ground for discussing two modern philosophical mistakes about the character and limits of human knowledge.

The solution, it seems to me, lies in recognizing the sense in which the word "knowledge" signifies something that is quite distinct from anything that can be called an opinion, and the sense in which a certain type of opinion can also quite properly be called knowledge. That would leave another type of opinion, quite distinct from knowledge, which should properly be called mere opinion.

When the criteria for calling anything knowledge are such exacting criteria as the certitude, incorrigibility, and immutability of the truth that is known, then the few things that are knowledge stand far apart from everything that might be called opinion.

Examples of knowledge in this extreme sense of the term are a small number of self-evident truths. A self-evident truth is one that states something the opposite of which it is impossible to think. It can also be called a necessary truth because its opposite is impossible.

That a finite whole is greater than any of its component parts and that each part of a finite whole is less than the whole are self-evident, necessary truths. We cannot think the opposite. The terms *part* and *whole* are indefinable. We cannot say what a part is without using the notion of whole, or what a whole is without using the notion of part, and so we cannot define either part or whole by itself. Neverthe-

*Six Great Ideas* (1981).

less, we do so understand what parts and wholes are in relation to one another, that we cannot understand a part being greater than a whole or a whole less than a part.

Sometimes definitions enter into our grasp of self-evident truths. We define a triangle as a three-sided plane figure. We define a diagonal as a line drawn between nonadjacent angles in a regular plane polygon. We know that, being three-sided, a triangle has no nonadjacent angles. Therefore, we know with certitude that it is necessarily true that there can be no diagonals in triangles, as there can be in squares, pentagons, and the like.

Whether they know it or not, those who say that we have precious little knowledge that has such certitude may not realize that the little knowledge we have of this kind consists of a handful of self-evident or necessary truths like those just noted.

Is everything else opinion, then? Yes and no; yes, if we insist upon the criteria of certitude, incorrigibility, and immutability of the truth known; no, if we relax those criteria and recognize that there are opinions we can affirm on the basis of evidence and reasons that have sufficient probative force to justify our claiming *at the time* that the opinion affirmed is true.

I stress "at the time" because, since we have given up the criteria of incorrigibility and immutability, we must be prepared to have the opinion we now claim to be true on the basis of the evidence and reasons now available turn out to be false in the future, or in need of correction or alteration at some future time when new evidence and other reasons come into play.

We should be prepared to say that such corrigible, mutable opinions are knowledge—knowledge of truths that have

a future in which they may undergo correction or alteration and even rejection. As against opinions that deserve
the status of knowledge in this sense of the term, there remain what must be called mere opinions because they are
asserted without any basis at all in evidence or reason.

Our personal prejudices are such mere opinions. We assert them stoutly and often stubbornly, even though we
cannot point to a single piece of evidence in support of them
or offer a single reason for claiming that they are true. This
is also true of some of the beliefs we harbor and cherish.

Sometimes we use the word "belief" to signify that we
have some measure of doubt about the opinion we claim to
be true on the basis of evidence and reasons. In that case,
it is not incorrect to say of one and the same thing that we
know it (because we have sufficient grounds for affirming
it to be true) and that we also believe it (because the grounds
we have still leave us with some trace of doubt about its
truth).

However, at other times, we use the word "belief" to
signify total lack of evidence or reasons for asserting an
opinion. What we believe goes beyond all available evidence and reasons *at the time*. Then we should never say
that we know, but only that we believe the mere opinion
that we are holding on to.

The only time when it is totally inappropriate to use the
word "belief" is in the case of self-evident or necessary
truths. We know that the whole is greater than any of its
parts. To say that we believe it is an egregious misunderstanding of the truth being affirmed. The same thing applies to many, but not all, mathematical truths. We know,
we do not believe, that two plus two equals four.

Not only personal prejudices but all matters of personal

taste, liking one thing and disliking another, fall in the realm of mere opinion. In such matters of taste or personal preference, we may have our own reasons for liking this and disliking that, but those reasons carry no weight with others whose likes and dislikes, or preferences, are contrary to our own.

The extension of the word "knowledge" to cover all corrigible and mutable opinions that can be asserted on the basis of evidence and reasons available at a given time covers more than opinions that can be affirmed beyond a reasonable doubt, if not beyond the shadow of a doubt. It includes opinions that have a preponderance of evidence or reasons in their favor as against opinions supported by weaker evidence or reasons.

In general it can be said that knowing is not like eating. When we eat something, we take it into our bodies, digest it, assimilate it. It becomes part of us. It no longer remains what it was before it was eaten. But with one striking exception, our knowing something in no way affects or alters the thing we know. We may take it into our minds in some way, but doing that leaves it exactly the same as it was before we knew it. The one exception occurs in the case of quantum mechanics, where the instruments we use to investigate the phenomena to be observed and measured do affect the phenomena as we observe and measure them.

What I have just said about the difference between knowing and eating requires me to call attention to another special use, or misuse, of the word "knowing." It involves the distinction between two acts of the mind to which I called attention in the preceding chapter.

The first act of the mind is simple apprehension. Some object is apprehended, be it a perceptual object, an object

of memory or imagination, or an object of conceptual thought. Strictly speaking, with one exception, we should not use the word "knowledge" for such apprehensions.

Except for perceptual apprehensions, which cannot be separated from perceptual judgments, all other apprehensions are totally devoid of any judgment about the object apprehended—whether or not it does exist, whether or not its character in fact is identical with its character as apprehended. Devoid of such judgments, an apprehension is not knowledge because there is nothing true or false about it. True and false enter the picture only with the act of judging, and only then do we go beyond apprehension to what, strictly speaking, can be called knowledge.

There is a sense in which knowing is like eating. The edible, before it is eaten, exists quite independently of the eater and is whatever it is regardless of how it is transformed by being eaten. So, too, the knowable exists quite independently of the knower and is whatever it is whether it is known or not, and however it is known.

The word that most of us use to signify the independent character of the knowable is the word "reality." If there were no reality, nothing the existence and character of which is independent of the knowing mind, there would be nothing knowable. Reality is that which exists whether we think about it or not, and has the character that it has no matter how we think about it.

The reality that is the knowable may or may not be physical. It may or may not consist solely of things perceptible to our senses. But whatever its character, its existence must be public, not private. It must be knowable by two or more persons. Nothing that is knowable by one person alone can have the status of knowledge. Whatever can be

genuinely known by any one person must be capable of being known by others.

Let this suffice as background for the discussion to follow. I will be using the word "knowledge" to cover the necessary and self-evident truths we know with certitude and also the opinions we are able to assert on the basis of sufficient evidence and reasons to outweigh any contrary opinions. I will be using it to cover things about which we can say both that we know them and also that we believe them, because some measure of doubt remains about them. I will be using it always for judgments that are either true or false, but never for apprehensions that are neither true nor false. And I will use the phrase "mere opinion" for whatever is deemed by anyone not to be knowledge in any of the foregoing senses.

## 2

The authors of the two philosophical mistakes with which we are here concerned are David Hume and Immanuel Kant. The influence that, historically, Hume had upon Kant, conceded by Kant to have prompted the philosophical edifice he constructed in order to avoid the conclusions reached by Hume (which he thought untenable, even disastrous), throws some light on the relation of the two mistakes.

Looked at one way, the two mistakes represent opposite extremes. Looked at another way, they represent opposite faces of the same error. The error in both cases has to do with the role that sense-experience plays with regard to the origin and limits of knowledge. The two mistakes are opposed to one another by reason of the fact that they take opposite stands with regard to the certitude, immutability,

and incorrigibility that does or does not belong to knowledge.

Hume's mistake had its roots or origin in earlier mistakes, the mistakes discussed in Chapters 1 and 2, and especially the mistakes made by John Locke with regard to the senses and the intellect and with regard to ideas as objects we directly apprehend. On the other hand, Kant's mistake had its origin in the mistake made by Hume. He might have avoided his own mistake by pointing out that the conclusions Hume reached, which he found so repugnant, were based on false premises.

Had he rejected those premises, that by itself would have sufficed to avoid Hume's conclusions. But he did not do so. Instead, he invented and erected a subtle and intricate philosophical structure in an effort to reach and support conclusions the very opposite of Hume's, and just as incorrect.

### 3

Let us begin with Hume and then go on to Kant. The place to begin is with the conclusion that Hume reached in the very closing pages of his *Enquiry Concerning Human Understanding*.

It is here that Hume proposes to adopt what he calls "a more mitigated skepticism" than the extreme form that denies that we can have any knowledge at all—that there is anything either true or false. Accordingly, he concedes that we do have knowledge of two sorts.

One is the kind of knowledge to be found in mathematics. He refers to this as "abstract science" because it involves no assertions or judgments about matters of fact or real existence. It deals only with the relation between our

own ideas—our ideas of quantity and number. Here it is possible to have demonstration and a measure of certitude. But, he goes on to say, "all attempts to extend this more perfect species of knowledge beyond these bounds are mere sophistry and illusion."

Our definitions of certain terms give us some propositions or judgments that also have a measure of certitude. Thus if we define injustice as a violation of property, then we can be certain that where there is no property, there can be no injustice. But this is just a matter of definition. Injustice can be defined differently, and so it is not intrinsically impossible to think that there can be injustice where there is no property.

Hume then tells us that, apart from mathematics, "all other enquiries of men regard only matters of fact and existence; and these are evidently incapable of demonstration." The opposite of any judgment that something exists or that it is such and such is always possible. Judgments about matters of fact and real existence can be supported by evidence and reasons. When they are, they constitute knowledge, not mere opinion; but they are always knowledge that lacks certitude and falls within the sphere of doubt—the sphere of the corrigible and the mutable.

Such knowledge depends upon our sense-experience. "It is only experience," Hume writes, "which teaches us the nature and bounds of cause and effect, and enables us to infer the existence of one object from that of another." According to these criteria, Hume admits into the sphere of empirical knowledge (as contrasted with abstract science) such things as history, geography, and astronomy, and also the sciences "which treat of general facts . . . politics, natural philosophy, physics, chemistry, etc."

This brings him to his thundering conclusion in the last paragraph of the *Enquiry:*

When we run over our libraries, persuaded of these principles, what havoc must we make? If we take in our hand any volume; of divinity or school metaphysics, for instance; let us ask, *Does it contain any abstract reasoning concerning quantity or number?* No. *Does it contain any experimental reasoning concerning matters of fact and existence?* No. Commit it then to the flames: for it can contain nothing but sophistry and illusion.

The line that divides what deserves to be honored and respected as genuine knowledge from what should be dismissed as mere opinion (or worse, as sophistry and illusion) is determined by two criteria. (1) It is knowledge and can be called science if it deals solely with abstractions and involves no judgments about matters of fact or real existence. Here we have mathematics and, together with it, the science of logic. (2) It is knowledge, if it deals with particular facts, as history and geography do, or with general facts, as physics and chemistry do.

In both cases, it is knowledge only to the extent that it is based upon experimental reasoning, involving empirical investigations of the kind that occur in laboratories and observatories, or methodical investigations of the kind conducted by historians and geographers.

What did Hume exclude from the realm of knowledge? Even though he refers to what he calls "natural philosophy," which in his century was identical with what we have come to call physical science, his intention was to reject as sophistry and illusion, or at least as mere opinion, what in antiquity and in the Middle Ages was traditional philosophy, including here a philosophy of nature, or physics

that is not experimental and does not rely on empirical investigations, as well as metaphysics and philosophical theology.

This view of knowledge and opinion comes down to us in the nineteenth and twentieth centuries in the form of a doctrine that has been variously called positivism or scientism. The word "positivism" derives its meaning from the fact that the experimental or investigative sciences, and other bodies of knowledge, such as history, that rely upon investigation and research, came to be called positive sciences.

Positivism, then, is the view that the only genuine knowledge of reality or of the world of observable phenomena (i.e., matters of fact and existence) is to be found in the positive sciences. Mathematics and logic are also genuine knowledge, but they are not knowledge of the world of observable phenomena, or of matters of fact and real existence. The twentieth-century form of scientism or positivism thus came to be called "logical positivism."

Here we have one facet of the mistake about knowledge and opinion, the other facet of which is to be found in Immanuel Kant's *Critique of Pure Reason*. The latter is by far the more serious and the more far-reaching in its consequences.

4

Kant tells us that David Hume awakened him from his dogmatic slumbers. His prior dogmatism, as well as Hume's skepticism, which Kant also found repugnant, was replaced by the critical philosophy that he developed. It is also sometimes called a transcendental philosophy because of its transcendence with regard to experience.

In order to understand this, it is necessary, first, to pay

attention to two distinctions that are operative in Kant's thinking. One is the distinction between the *a priori* and the *a posteriori*. The other is the distinction between the *analytic* and the *synthetic*.

The *a priori*, according to Kant, includes whatever is in the mind prior to any sense-experience and also whatever judgments it can make that are not based upon sense-experience. The *a posteriori* is, of course, the opposite in both respects.

The *analytic* consists of judgments the truth of which depends entirely upon definitions. Thus, if lead is defined as a nonconducting metal, then the judgment that lead does not conduct electricity is an analytically true judgment. So, too, if man is defined as a rational animal, the judgment that men have reason is analytically true. In each example, the term that is predicated of the subject being considered ("does not conduct electricity" and "have reason") is already contained within the definition of the subject being considered ("lead" and "men").

Clearly, such analytical judgments can be, in fact must be, *a priori*. Their truth depends solely upon a definition of terms, not upon sense-experience. Hume would have regarded such analytical judgments as truths that deal with the relation of our own ideas, not with matters of fact and existence. John Locke, before him, regarded them as mere verbal tautologies; in his words, judgments that are "trifling and uninstructive." Locke, in my judgment, is correct in dismissing them as unworthy of serious consideration.

Earlier in this chapter, I explained the character of self-evident truths, truths that have certitude and incorrigibility because it is impossible for us to think their opposites. Such a truth as *a finite whole is greater than any of its parts*

is not analytical in Kant's sense: its focal terms—whole and part—are indefinable. Nor is it *a priori* in Kant's sense: its truth depends upon our understanding of the terms *whole* and *part*, an understanding that is derived from a single experience, such as tearing a piece of paper into pieces, thus dividing a whole into parts.

Philosophers since Kant have misconceived what an earlier tradition in philosophy had understood to be self-evident truths or axioms. They have mistakenly accepted Kant's restriction of such truths to verbal tautologies, to trifling and uninstructive statements.

But this is not the worst of Kant's mistakes. Much worse is his view about synthetic judgments *a priori*. A synthetic judgment is not trifling or uninstructive. It does not depend upon an arbitrary definition of terms. It is the kind of judgment that Hume regarded as a truth about matters of fact or real existence. In every such case, the opposite of what is asserted is possible—thinkable, conceivable. But for Hume, the very fact that a judgment is synthetic involves its dependence on experience of one sort or another. It cannot, therefore, be *a priori*—independent of sense-experience.

To maintain that there are synthetic judgments *a priori*, as Kant does, is, perhaps, the single most revolutionary step that he took to overcome the conclusions reached by Hume that he found repugnant. What was his driving purpose in doing so? It was to establish Euclidean geometry and traditional arithmetic as sciences that not only have certitude, but also contain truths that are applicable to the world of our experience. It was also to give the same status to Newtonian physics.

To do this, Kant endowed the human mind with tran-

scendental forms of sense-apprehension or intuition (the forms of space and time), and also with the transcendental categories of the understanding. These are not to be confused with Descartes' "innate ideas." The mind brings these transcendental forms and categories to experience, thereby constituting the shape and character of the experience we have.

According to Kant, the mind is not (as John Locke rightly insisted it was in his refutation of Cartesian innate ideas) a *tabula rasa*—a total blank—until it acquires ideas initially from sense-experience. Locke rightly subscribed to the mediaeval maxim that there is nothing in the mind that does not somehow derive from sense-experience. It was this maxim that Kant rejected.

The transcendental forms of sense-apprehension and the transcendental categories of the understanding are inherent in the mind and constitute its structure prior to any sense-experience. The common experience that all of us share has the character it does have because it has been given that character by the transcendental structure of the human mind. It has been formed and constituted by it.

This elaborate machinery invented by Kant enabled him to think that he had succeeded in establishing and explaining the certitude and incorrigibility of Euclidean geometry, simple arithmetic, and Newtonian physics. Three historic events suffice to show how illusory is the view that he had succeeded in doing that.

The discovery and development of the non-Euclidean geometries and of modern number theory should suffice to show how utterly factitious was Kant's invention of the transcendental forms of space and time as controlling our sense-apprehensions and giving certitude and reality to

Euclidean geometry and simple arithmetic.

Similarly, the replacement of Newtonian physics by modern relativistic physics, the addition of probabilistic or statistical laws to causal laws, the development of elementary particle physics and of quantum mechanics, should also suffice to show how utterly factitious was Kant's invention of the transcendental categories of the understanding to give Newtonian physics certitude and incorrigibility.

How anyone in the twentieth century can take Kant's transcendental philosophy seriously is baffling, even though it may always remain admirable in certain respects as an extraordinarily elaborate and ingenious intellectual invention.

So much for the illusory character of what Kant claimed for his transcendental philosophy as an attempt to give mathematics and natural science a certitude and incorrigibility that they do not possess. What about the critical character that Kant claimed for his philosophy—critical in the sense that it would save us from the dogmatism of traditional metaphysics, especially its cosmology and natural theology?

Kant argues for the exclusion of traditional metaphysics from the realm of genuine knowledge on the grounds that it must employ concepts derived from experience to make assertions that go beyond experience—the experience that is constituted by the *a priori* structure of the human mind. Where Hume dismissed traditional metaphysics as sophistry or illusion, Kant dismissed it as trans-empirical.

However, all the ideas used in metaphysics are not empirical concepts. The idea of God, for example, and the idea of the cosmos as a whole are not concepts derived from sense-experience. They are instead theoretical constructs.

There is, therefore, nothing invalid about employing such an idea even if it goes beyond all the sense-experience available to us. Let me add here that, unlike an empirical concept, a theoretical construct does not and cannot have any perceived particular instances.

What I have just said about such metaphysical concepts as God and the cosmos as a whole applies equally to some of the most important ideas in twentieth-century theoretical physics, such ideas as the idea of quark, of certain elementary particles, such as mesons, or of black holes. All of these are theoretical constructs, not empirical concepts.

Kant had no awareness of the distinction between empirical concepts and theoretical constructs. His reasons for dismissing traditional metaphysics as devoid of the validity appropriate to genuine knowledge would apply equally to much of twentieth-century physics. Here, once more, we have grounds for not taking much stock in Kant's claims for the critical character of his philosophy.

Finally, we come to what is, perhaps, the most serious mistake that modern philosophy inherited from Kant—the mistake of substituting idealism for realism. Even though Locke and his successor Hume made the mistake of thinking that the ideas in our minds are the only objects we directly apprehend, they somehow (albeit not without contradicting themselves) regarded us as having knowledge of a reality that is independent of our minds. Not so with Kant.

The valid knowledge that we have is always and only knowledge of a world we experience. But precisely because it is a world as experienced by us, it is not, according to Kant, a world independent of our minds. It is not independent, as we have already seen, because experience is

constituted by the transcendental or *a priori* structure of our minds—its forms of intuition or apprehension and its categories of understanding. Not being independent of our minds, it can hardly be regarded as reality, for the essential characteristic of the real is independence of the human mind.

For Kant the only things that are independent of the human mind are, in his words, *"Dinge an sich"*—things in themselves that are intrinsically unknowable. This is tantamount to saying that the real is the unknowable, and the knowable is ideal in the sense that it is invested with the ideas that our minds bring to it to make it what it is.

The positivism or scientism that has its roots in Hume's philosophical mistakes, and the idealism and critical constraints that have their roots in Kant's philosophical mistakes, generate many embarrassing consequences that have plagued modern thought since their day. In almost every case, the trouble has consisted in the fact that later thinkers tried to avoid the consequences without correcting the errors or mistakes that generated them.

In this short chapter, it is impossible to deal with the shortcomings, embarrassments, and additional errors in nineteenth- and twentieth-century thought. I will confine myself to a brief treatment of knowledge and opinion that corrects and avoids the philosophical mistakes made by Hume and Kant.

5

Let us return to the focal point of this discussion—the distinction between knowledge and mere opinion. On the one hand, we have self-evident truths that have certitude and incorrigibility; and we also have truths that are still subject

to doubt but that are supported by evidence and reasons to a degree that puts them beyond reasonable doubt or at least gives them predominance over contrary views. All else is mere opinion—with no claim to being knowledge or having any hold on truth.

There is no question that the findings and conclusions of historical research are knowledge in this sense; no question that the findings and conclusions of the experimental or empirical sciences, both natural and social, are knowledge in this sense.

As contrasted with such knowledge, which is knowledge of reality or, as Hume would say, knowledge of matters of fact and real existence, mathematics and logic are also knowledge, but not of reality. They are not experimental or empirical knowledge. They do not depend upon investigative research for their findings and conclusions.

The question that remains to be answered is the one that, in my judgment, Hume and Kant answered erroneously, an answer that has persisted in various forms down to our own day. Where does speculative or theoretical philosophy (by which I mean philosophical physics, metaphysics, and philosophical theology) stand in this picture? Is it mere opinion or is it genuine knowledge, knowledge that, like the empirical sciences, is knowledge of reality?

According to Sir Karl Popper, one of the most eminent philosophers of science in our time, the line of demarcation between knowledge and mere opinion is determined by one criterion: falsifiability by empirical evidence, by observed phenomena. An opinion, a view, a theory, that cannot be thus falsified is not knowledge, but mere opinion, neither true nor false in any objective sense of those terms. Drawing this line of demarcation, Popper places the

experimental and empirical sciences on one side of the line, and theoretical philosophy (covering what I have indicated above) on the other side of the line.

Though it is couched in somewhat different terms, Popper thus repeats the conclusion Hume reached in his *Enquiry*. The reasons for reaching the opposite conclusion are as follows.

In the first place, what has been overlooked is the distinction between common and special experience. The empirical evidence to which science and history appeal is evidence that consists in observed data produced by methodical investigation, using all the devices and instrumentation of the laboratory and the observatory. Such observed data are no part of the experience of ordinary individuals who do not engage in scientific or historical investigation.

In sharp contrast to such special experience, available only to those who engage in investigation, there is the everyday, ordinary experience that all of us have during the waking hours of our life. This experience comes to us simply by our being awake and having our senses acted on. We make no effort to get it; we are not seeking to answer questions by means of it; we employ no methods to refine it; we use no instruments of observation to obtain it. Within the range of such experience there lies a core that constitutes the common experience of mankind—experience that is the same for all human beings at all times and places.

With this distinction in mind, between special and common experience, between experience resulting from investigation efforts and experience enjoyed without such efforts, we can distinguish between bodies of knowledge that, while depending on experience as well as upon reflective thought, rely on different types of experience.

Mathematics is a case in point. Mathematical research is carried on mainly by reflective and analytical thought, but it also relies on some experience—the common experience that all human beings have. Mathematicians do not engage in empirical investigation. They need no special data of observation. Mathematics can be called an armchair science, and yet some experience—the common experience of mankind—lies behind the reflective and analytical thought in which the mathematician engages.

Speculative or theoretical philosophy, like mathematics, is a body of knowledge that can be produced in an armchair or at a desk. The only experience that the philosopher needs for the development of his theories or the support of his conclusions is the common experience of mankind. Reflecting on such experience and proceeding by means of rational analysis and argument, the philosopher reaches conclusions in a manner that resembles the procedure of the mathematician, not that of the empirical scientist.

However, we must not fail to note one important difference, a difference that aligns the theoretical philosopher with the empirical scientist rather than with the mathematician. Unlike mathematics, but like empirical science, theoretical philosophy claims to be knowledge of reality.

In the light of what has just been said, we can divide the sphere of knowledge into (1) bodies of knowledge that are methodically investigative and (2) bodies of knowledge that are noninvestigative and that employ only common, not special, experience. To the first group belong history, geography, and all the empirical sciences, both natural and social. To the second group belong mathematics, logic, and theoretical philosophy.

If the division is made in terms of whether the body of

knowledge claims to have a hold on truth about reality, then theoretical philosophy, even though it is noninvestigative in method, belongs with history, geography, and the empirical sciences.

Each of these disciplines, according to its distinctive character, has a method peculiarly its own and, according to the limitations of that method, can answer only certain questions, not others. The kind of questions that the philosopher or the mathematician can answer without any empirical investigation whatsoever cannot be answered by the empirical scientist, and, conversely, the kind of questions that the scientist can answer by his methods of investigation cannot be answered by the philosopher or the mathematician.

The line of demarcation between all these bodies of knowledge and mere opinion involves criteria other than the one proposed by Popper. Falsifiability by experience—whether it be the observed data of scientific investigation or the substance of common experience—is certainly one criterion by which we separate genuine knowledge from mere opinion. But it is not the only one.

Another is refutability by rational argument. The only irrefutable truths we possess are the very few self-evident propositions that have certitude, finality, incorrigibility. Since our knowledge of reality, whether scientific or philosophical, does not consist exclusively of self-evident truths nor does it consist of conclusions demonstrated to be true by deduction from premises that are self-evidently true, scientific and philosophical theories or conclusions must be refutable in three ways.

One way is falsification by experience, which produces evidence contrary to the evidence that has been employed

to support the opinion that claims to be true and to have the status of knowledge. A second way is by rational argument, which advances reasons that correct and replace the reasons advanced to support the opinion that claims to be true and have the status of knowledge. The third way is a combination of the first and the second—new and better evidence, together with new and better reasons for holding a view contrary to the one that has been refuted.

Opinions that cannot be refuted in one or another of these three ways are not knowledge, but mere opinion.

Were this not so, this book would be fraudulent in its claim to point out philosophical mistakes and to correct them by offering evidence and reasons to expose their errors. Nor could we replace them with views that are true or more nearly true.

If philosophy were mere opinion there would be no philosophical mistakes, erroneous views, false doctrines. There would be no way of substituting views or doctrines more nearly true because they employed insights and appealed to distinctions that for one reason or another were not in the possession of those who made the mistakes.

6

The foregoing analysis has not been exhaustive. It does not include bodies of knowledge that result from scholarly research in fields such as philology, the comparative study of religion, or the fine arts. If these bodies of knowledge rely upon methodical investigation they belong with the empirical sciences, not philosophy. The other question to be decided is whether or not they are knowledge of reality.

Reference to religious belief or faith has also been omitted. It claims to be knowledge and would lose all its effi-

cacy if it were reduced to mere opinion. But the grounds on which it makes such a claim are so utterly different from the criteria we have employed to divide genuine knowledge from mere opinion that it is impossible within the brief scope of this discussion to put religious faith or belief into the picture we now have before us.

On the basis of the common experience that all of us possess, we have common-sense knowledge about matters of fact and real existence, knowledge that is neither scientific nor philosophical. There is, however, a relation between such common-sense knowledge and theoretical philosophy that does not exist between it and empirical science.

Theoretical philosophy is an analytical and reflective refinement of what we know by common sense in the light of common experience. Our common-sense knowledge is deepened, illuminated, and elaborated by philosophical thought. There is little if any sound philosophy that conflicts with our common-sense knowledge, for both are based on the common human experience out of which they emerge.

That is why I have reiterated again and again that philosophy, unlike the investigative sciences, historical research, or mathematics, is everybody's business. All the latter are fields that tend toward greater and greater specialization and become the province of a wide variety of specialist experts. Philosophy alone, because of its intimate connection with the common-sense knowledge of the ordinary individual, remains unspecialized—the province of the generalist, the business of everybody.

The importance of refuting the errors made by Hume and Kant, errors that are widely prevalent in the twentieth

century, is that the relegation of theoretical philosophy to the realm of mere opinion amounts to a cultural disaster in an age that is so dominated by increasing specialization in all other fields of learning. If philosophical speculation is not respected in its claim to have a hold upon the truth about reality, our culture will cease to have generalists.

Knowledge is not the highest of the intellectual goods. Of higher value is understanding and, beyond that, wisdom. These are goods that, to whatever extent they can be achieved, become ours through philosophical thought, not scientific knowledge. Philosophy makes its contribution not only as a body of knowledge, but also because it is through philosophical thought that we are able to understand everything else that we know. We are justified in hoping that from such understanding, with maturity of judgment and wide experience, some measure of wisdom will ultimately be attained.

# CHAPTER 5
# Moral Values

## 1

IN THE PRECEDING CHAPTER we dealt with knowledge of reality—of matters of fact and real existence. In that connection we considered the status of speculative or theoretical philosophy that claims to be knowledge of reality.

The question we face here is whether there is another kind of knowledge, such as moral philosophy, that does not claim to be knowledge of reality but rather is concerned with moral values—with good and evil, right and wrong, with what we ought to seek in our lives, and what we ought or ought not to do.

Clearly there is a chasm between judgments about what does or does not exist, or about what are or are not the characteristics of some existent thing, and judgments about what ought or ought not to be sought or what ought or ought not to be done. The first type of judgment, involving as-

sertions that are existential or characterizing, let us call descriptive. The second type, involving *oughts* or *ought nots*, let us call prescriptive. Sometimes, the latter are also called normative because they lay down standards or norms of conduct.

The chasm referred to above is the chasm between matters of fact on the one hand, and questions of value on the other hand, especially such values as good and evil, right and wrong. Judgments about these matters are intimately related to the type of judgment that I have just called prescriptive or normative. If one thinks that something is really good, that is tantamount to saying that it ought to be sought. So, too, if one thinks that something is really right to do, that is tantamount to saying that it ought to be done.

If people generally were asked where they stand on the question whether moral philosophy is genuine knowledge that has a hold on truth about moral values, we would find, I think, that they divide into two groups. I would not hazard a guess about which group represents a clear majority, but my guess is that neither one greatly outweighs the other.

One group consists of those who think that when we are dealing with reality, with matters of fact and real existence, we do have genuine knowledge and have some hold on truth, even though that truth may be subject to doubt and correction. But in their view, our judgments of value about good and evil, right and wrong, or our prescriptive judgments about what ought or ought not to be done, are neither true nor false. They express nothing but our personal preferences, our likes and dislikes.

For this group moral philosophy is not a body of genuine knowledge. Moral judgments are just mere opinion, concerning which there is no point in arguing, as there is

no point in arguing about any matters of taste or personal predilection. When confronting disputes about moral values, this group dismisses them as pointless, repeating the oft-repeated remark that one man's meat is another man's poison. They may even quote Montaigne or Shakespeare to the effect that there is nothing good or evil but thinking makes it so.

The other group takes the diametrically opposite view. For them there are absolute and universal standards of right and wrong, of what ought to be done or ought not to be done. They do not engage in argument about such matters, for they feel secure in their dogmatic assertion that the existence of objective moral values and standards is incontrovertible. They sometimes call themselves the moral majority, but whether they are majority or minority, they are a considerable part of the population.

There is little if any genuine debate or dispute between these two groups. Each, for its own reasons, would regard any attempt to resolve the issue between them as utterly futile. To that extent, both are equally dogmatic. The first group would be unable to defend its subjectivistic and relativistic attitude toward moral values, if that view were critically challenged. The second group would be unable to support the opposite view by rational arguments. It might appeal to articles of religious faith, but that is as far as it could go.

Before I proceed, let me make sure that all of us understand as clearly as possible the meaning of such terms as *subjective* and *relative*, on the one hand, and such terms as *objective* and *absolute*, on the other hand.

The subjective is that which differs for you, for me, and for everyone else. In contrast, the objective is that which

is the same for you, for me, and for everyone else.

The relative is that which varies from time to time and alters with alterations in the circumstances. In contrast, the absolute is that which does not vary from time to time and does not alter with alterations in the circumstances.

On one side of the issue about moral values and prescriptive judgments are those persons who hold that they are subjective and relative. On the other side of the issue are those persons who hold that they are objective and absolute.

Not just people generally, but philosophers have been divided on this issue. The philosophical mistakes with which this chapter is concerned assert, for different reasons, that moral values and prescriptive judgments are subjective and relative. One of these mistakes, the hedonist error of identifying the good with pleasure, is ancient as well as modern. The rest are distinctively modern in origin.

Those among people generally who hold the view that moral values and prescriptive judgments are subjective and relative are not acquainted with the philosophical mistakes that underlie their view. These mistakes have filtered down to them and have penetrated their minds without their being explicitly aware of them.

Those among people generally who so dogmatically hold the opposite view are equally unaware of the insights, distinctions, and arguments by which the view they hold can be rationally defended and supported. They do not know how, by reason and argument, they can correct the errors made by their opponents.

With all this in mind, I propose to proceed as follows. I will, first, attempt to state the hedonist error, which is both ancient and modern; and then turn to the more fundamen-

tal mistake that modern thought has inherited from David Hume, a mistake that Immanuel Kant tried to correct but failed to do so because he went too far in the opposite direction.

Having done that, I will, in a succeeding section, attempt to expose what lies at the root of these mistakes, particularly those of modern origin. Finally, I will briefly and in summary fashion state what I think are the serious consequences of subjectivism and relativism with regard to moral values, and the importance of correcting the philosophical mistakes that cause them.

## 2

The popular and vulgar version of hedonism leads its exponents to be subjectivists and relativists about moral values. Identifying the good with pleasure, it is an easy step to conclude that what is deemed good by one individual because it gives pleasure may not be deemed good by another. The pleasures human beings experience vary from individual to individual, from time to time, and with variations in the circumstances.

But once critical questions are asked and distinctions are made, the hedonist position as popularly held ceases to be tenable. To say that the *only* good is pleasure is to say that wealth, health, friends, knowledge, and wisdom are not good. This, in turn, means that they are neither desirable nor in fact desired by anyone, for certainly whatever is desirable or desired is in some sense good. The facts of everyday life thus make it impossible to maintain that the *only* thing everyone in fact desires or regards as desirable is pleasure.

It was in this way that Plato, in his dialogue *Philebus*, argued against the sophistical view that pleasure and good are the same. If a life that includes both pleasure and wisdom is more desirable than one that includes pleasure alone, then pleasure is not the *only* good.

In a similar manner Aristotle, in the tenth book of his *Nicomachean Ethics*, argued against Eudoxus. Pleasure accompanies our activities, he wrote, but "the pleasure proper to a worthy activity is good and that proper to an unworthy activity is bad."

In antiquity, Epicurus and his followers started out being simpleminded hedonists by affirming boldly that pleasure and the good are identical, but as they proceeded to delineate the features of a good life, it soon became apparent that other things are desirable and even more desirable than pleasure. They distinguished between lower and higher pleasures, the pleasures of the intellect being, in their view, more desirable than the pleasures of the senses. But in order to maintain such a distinction the Epicureans must have had some standard of goodness other than pleasure in and of itself.

In the modern world the leading self-avowed hedonist is John Stuart Mill who, in his *Utilitarianism*, acknowledges Epicurus and Epicureanism to be his precursor. But, like Epicurus, Mill cannot long maintain the simpleminded view that the only good is pleasure. He, too, distinguishes between pleasures that are more or less desirable.

"There is no known Epicurean theory of life," Mill writes, "which does not assign to the pleasures of the intellect, of the feelings and the imagination and of moral sentiments, a much higher value as pleasures than those of mere sensation." And, in one very famous passage, he adds:

[ 113 ]

It is better to be a human being dissatisfied than a pig satisfied; better to be Socrates dissatisfied than a fool satisfied. And if the fool, or the pig, are of a different opinion, it is because they only know their own side of the question. The other party to the comparison knows both sides.

That passage contains two words, "satisfied" and "dissatisfied," which hold the key to the untenability of simpleminded hedonism. People in general who are hedonists and also philosophers such as Epicurus and Mill who claim to be hedonists ignore a distinction that changes the picture radically. It is the distinction between sensual pleasures as objects of desire and the pleasure we call satisfaction when any of our desires are fulfilled.

Sensual pleasures cannot be identified with the good, for sensual pleasures are certainly not the only things we desire, nor do we always find them more desirable than other things, for the procurement of which we are even willing to suffer pain. On the other hand, the pleasure we experience whenever any of our desires is satisfied—the pleasure that is identical with the satisfaction of desire—is an accompaniment of the good, but not identical with it.

Let the good be wealth, health, friends, knowledge, or wisdom, or let it be sensual pleasure. When this or that good is desired by us and we succeed in obtaining the object of our desire, we experience the pleasure that consists in having our desire satisfied.

When Epicurus or Mill talk about lower and higher pleasures, they are in fact talking about lower and higher goods—about wisdom as a higher good than sensual pleasure, for example. The pleasure or satisfaction that we experience in obtaining a higher rather than a lower good is thus itself a higher pleasure or greater satisfaction.

The distinction between the two senses of the word "pleasure"—referring to sensual pleasures, on the one hand, and to the satisfaction of any desire, on the other hand—makes simpleminded hedonism untenable. But it does not solve the problem of moral values: whether they are objective and universal, or subjective and relative.

In the first place, we cannot find in Epicurus or Mill the basis for ordering goods as higher and lower, or for showing that what some individuals deem to be higher goods should be deemed so by everyone else at all times and places and under all circumstances.

Mill condemns individuals "who pursue sensual indulgences to the injury of health, though perfectly aware that health is the greater good." But does this include all individuals, or just some? What about those who seek sensual pleasures at the sacrifice of their health, regarding the former not the latter as the greater good? How do we advance rational arguments to persuade them that they are wrong—that everyone *ought* to prefer health to sensual pleasure because it is the greater good? And is this *ought*—the prescriptive statement—objectively and universally true?

These are questions to which we cannot find a satisfactory answer in Epicurus or Mill. While they may have been forced by their own common sense to abandon their initial simpleminded hedonism, they are not out of the woods. Identifying the good with the desirable rather than with pleasure in either of its two senses still leaves them unprotected against subjectivism and relativism.

Why? Because individuals differ in their desires, and so what is desired by one individual may not be desired by another, what is desired at one time or under certain circumstances may not be desired at another time and under

other circumstances. What is good or evil thus shifts from one individual to another, from one time to another, from one set of circumstances to another.

It was Spinoza, at the beginning of modern times, who advanced the view that whatever anyone desires *appears* good to that individual as a consequence of his desiring it. Whatever in fact we desire we call good. Good, Spinoza maintained, is nothing but the name attached to whatever objects we happen to desire. We deem them good *because* we desire them, not the other way around—desiring them *because* they are in fact good.

Unless Spinoza can be shown to be wrong, there is no way of escaping the subjectivism and relativism that inexorably follows from identifying the good with that which is consciously desired by anyone or explicitly thought to be desirable by them. As actual desires or opinions about the desirable shift from person to person and from time to time, the judgment that anything is or is not good remains a subjective, personal predilection, and is relative to time and circumstances.

While it is true that Spinoza, like Epicurus before him and Mill after him, propounded ethical theories in which certain goods are stoutly proclaimed to be higher or better than others, not just for this or that individual but for every human being and under all circumstances, they do not have in their ethics or moral philosophy grounds adequate for establishing the truth of such views, as against the subjectivism and relativism that they cannot overcome because of other things they either say or fail to say.

Adequate grounds can be found, but I will postpone stating them until we have faced an even more serious at-

tack on the validity of moral philosophy and on its legitimacy as genuine knowledge rather than mere opinion.

## 3

The origin of that more serious attack is to be found in David Hume's *Treatise on Human Nature* in the eighteenth century. In a famous passage, Hume points out that, in his reading of works dealing with questions of morality, he is often surprised to find that their authors shift from saying what is or is not the case in reality to making assertions about what ought or ought not to be done in the conduct of human life. He then goes on to say:

As this *ought* or *ought not* expresses some new relation of affirmation, it is necessary that it should be observed and explained; and at the same time that a reason should be given for what seems altogether inconceivable, how this new relation can be a deduction from others, which are entirely different from it. I shall presume to recommend it to the readers; and am persuaded that this small attention would subvert all the vulgar systems of morality.

Let me explicate the important point that Hume is here making, about which he is not entirely incorrect. Calling attention to the distinction between descriptive statements (involving assertions of what is or is not) and prescriptive statements (involving assertions of what ought or ought not to be done), Hume rightly declares that the former type of statement cannot provide us with adequate grounds for validly and cogently reaching a conclusion that consists of the latter type of statement.

Even if the premises we were to employ consisted of complete knowledge of matters of fact and real existence

(the whole set of true "is" statements about reality), we could not validly argue from those premises to a single prescriptive or normative conclusion. In pointing this out, Hume is entirely correct. A prescriptive conclusion cannot be validly drawn from premises that are entirely descriptive.

Is there any way out of this? Can we find grounds for affirming the truth of prescriptive conclusions? The answer is yes if we can find a way of combining a prescriptive with a descriptive premise as the basis of our reasoning to a conclusion. Hume did not, could not, find that way of solving the problem and, because of that failure, he is responsible for the skepticism about the objective truth of moral philosophy that is prevalent in the twentieth century.

The skepticism that I have in mind goes by the name of "noncognitive ethics." That is an elegant way of saying that ethics or moral philosophy does not have the status of genuine knowledge. It consists solely of opinions that express our likes and dislikes, our preferences or predilections, our wishes or aversions, and even the commands we give to others. As Bertrand Russell once wittily said, "Ethics is the art of recommending to others what they must do to get along with ourselves."

The content of noncognitive ethics, consisting of mere opinions of this sort, is neither true nor false. What holds for mere opinions of any kind holds for mere opinions about moral values and about oughts. They are entirely subjective and relative to time and to changing circumstances.

One argument in favor of noncognitive ethics stems from Hume's critical point that our knowledge of reality, no

matter how much of it we have and no matter how sound it is, cannot by itself establish the truth of a single prescriptive judgment. However, that is not the only argument. There is another critical point that tends to remove prescriptive judgments from the sphere of truth and put them in the realm of mere opinions that are neither true nor false.

This point is made by a twentieth-century English philosopher, A. J. Ayer, as well as by others in his circle. It appeals to the correspondence theory of truth. We have truth in our minds when what we think agrees with the way things are. The ancient formulation of this theory declared that we have a hold on truth when we assert that that which is, is, and that which is not, is not; and we suffer falsehood when we assert that that which is, is not, or when we assert that that which is not, is.

This correspondence theory of truth, of the agreement of the mind with reality, obviously applies only to descriptive statements—statements that involve assertions about what is or is not. Just as obviously it does not apply to prescriptive statements. When we say that something ought or ought not to be done, what in reality can that correspond to? Clearly nothing; and so if the only kind of truth is the kind defined by the correspondence theory of truth, then prescriptive statements cannot be either true or false.

It is with this in mind that A. J. Ayer writes:

If a sentence makes no statement at all, there is obviously no sense in asking whether what it says is either true or false. And as we have seen, sentences which simply express moral judgments do not say anything. They are purely expressions of feeling and as such do not come under the category of truth and falsehood. They

are unverifiable for the same reasons that a cry of pain or a word of command is unverifiable—because they do not express genuine propositions.

Ayer goes further than he needs to go in order to support his thesis that ethics is noncognitive. There is no ground for saying that the sentence "Human beings ought to seek knowledge" asserts nothing at all. The fact that the sentence is prescriptive (an "ought" sentence) rather than descriptive (an "is" sentence) does not justify Ayer in dismissing the sentence as making no statement or assertion at all.

However, Ayer is justified in dismissing the prescriptive or "ought" statement as neither true nor false if the only kind of truth consists in the agreement of the mind with reality, for there are no matters of fact or real existence with which a prescriptive judgment can agree.

We have now pinpointed the three main supports for the widely prevalent view, among philosophers as well as among people generally, that moral values and prescriptive judgments are entirely subjective and relative.

One is Spinoza's identification of the good with that which appears good to the individual or that which the individual deems to be good or calls good simply and wholly *because* the object deemed or called good is consciously desired by the individual.

A second is Hume's criticism of anyone who tries to argue for a prescriptive conclusion on the basis solely of his knowledge of matters of fact or real existence. That cannot be done, as Hume correctly points out.

The third is the point made by the twentieth-century exponents of noncognitive ethics. If the only kind of truth is

to be found in descriptive statements that conform to the way things really are, they are then correct in excluding prescriptive or "ought" statements from the realm of what is either true or false.

With regard to the first point, we shall see that the error it involves can be removed by calling attention to another relation between the good and desire than the one considered by Spinoza. This involves a distinction between two kinds of desire, with which modern philosophers from Spinoza to Mill and others do not seem to be acquainted.

With regard to the second point, we shall see that it is possible to combine a prescriptive with a descriptive premise in order cogently to argue for the truth of a prescriptive conclusion. That prescriptive premise must, of course, be a self-evident truth; for otherwise we would have to argue for it and would be unable to do so.

With regard to the third point, we shall see that there is a kind of truth other than the kind of truth that applies solely to descriptive statements—a kind of truth that does not involve the agreement of the mind with reality. It was only in antiquity and in the Middle Ages that this distinction between two kinds of truth—one, descriptive truth; the other, prescriptive truth—was recognized and understood. Almost all modern philosophers are totally unaware of it.

In the following section I will explain how the problems raised by the three foregoing points are to be solved, thus correcting the philosophical mistakes that lead to subjectivism and relativism in regard to moral values and prescriptive judgments. But before I do so, I wish to spend a moment on Kant's attempt to avoid such subjectivism and relativism, an attempt which, in my judgment, fails be-

cause it goes too far in the opposite direction.

Admittedly, an error with regard to the relation between the good and the desirable is, in part, responsible for subjectivism and relativism. We acknowledge that an error with regard to the relation between value judgments and judgments about matters of fact is also in part responsible for this. One other thing that is in part responsible is a failure to answer the question about how prescriptive judgments can be true.

Kant's solution of these problems goes too far in the opposite direction because Kant tries to make moral duty or obligation, expressed in prescriptive or "ought judgments," totally independent of our desires and totally devoid of any reference to matters of fact, especially the facts about human nature. His categorical imperative is a prescriptive statement that he regards as a moral law by which our reason must be bound because it is self-evidently true.

In the first place, it is not self-evidently true. In the second place, it boils down to the golden rule which, however revered, is an empty recommendation. To say that one should do unto others what one wishes them to do unto oneself leaves totally unanswered the pivotal question: *What ought one rightly to wish others to do unto one's self?* That question cannot be answered without reference to our desires and the facts of human nature, which Kant excludes entirely from consideration.

Finally, Kant's assertion that the only thing that is really good is a good will, a will that obeys the categorical imperative and discharges its moral obligations accordingly, flies in the face of the facts. To identify the good with a good will violates facts with which we are all acquainted, as much as to identify the good with sensuous pleasure.

4

I will now address myself to the three critical points that pose problems to be solved. But I will not proceed in the same order in which those points were set forth in the preceding section.

Instead, I will deal first with the special kind of truth that is appropriate to prescriptive judgments. I will then introduce a distinction between two types of desires that relates to a distinction between the real and the apparent good. This will lay the ground for the formulation of the one and only prescriptive judgment that has self-evident truth. It serves as the requisite first principle of moral philosophy and enables us to draw prescriptive conclusions from premises that combine prescriptive and descriptive truths.

In Book VI of his *Nicomachean Ethics,* Aristotle, clearly cognizant of what he himself had said about the character of descriptive truth, declared that what he called practical judgments (i.e., prescriptive or normative judgments with respect to action) had truth of a different sort. Later philosophers, except for Aristotle's mediaeval disciples, have shown no awareness whatsoever of this brief but crucially important passage in his writings.

In the case of practical or prescriptive judgments, the requisite conformity that makes them true is conformity with right desire, not with the way things are, as is the case with descriptive truth. But what is right desire? Clearly, the answer must be that right desire consists in seeking what we ought to desire or seek. What ought we to desire? The answer cannot simply be the good, for whatever we desire has the aspect of the good whether or not our desires are right or wrong.

This brings us to the distinction between two kinds of

desire—natural, on the one hand, and acquired, on the other hand. Our natural desires are those inherent in our nature and consequently are the same in all members of the human species, all of whom have the same nature. In contrast, our acquired desires differ from individual to individual, according to their individual differences in temperament and according to the different circumstances of their upbringing and the different conditions that affect their development.

Two English words aptly express this distinction between natural and acquired desires. One is "needs"; the other, "wants." The introduction of these words carries connotations that everyone will recognize as involved in our use of them.

Whatever we need is really good for us. There are no wrong needs. We never need anything to an excess that is really bad for us. The needs that are inherent in our nature are all right desires. We can say, therefore, that a prescriptive judgment has practical truth if it expresses a desire for a good that we need.

In contrast to our natural needs, our individual wants lead us sometimes to seek what may appear to be good for us at the time but may turn out to be really bad for us. We all know that some of our acquired wants may be wrong desires and that we often want to excess something that is really good for us. The good that corresponds to our wants is, as wanted, only an apparent good that may turn out either to be really good for us or really bad for us, depending on whether we happen to want what we need or want something that interferes with or frustrates getting what we need.

Spinoza, it will be recalled, said that "good" is the name we give to the things we consciously desire. Those objects

*appear* good to us simply *because* we actually desire them. Since the acquired desires or wants of one individual tend to differ from the wants of another, what *appears* good to different individuals will differ.

In contrast to such apparent goods, real goods are the things all of us by nature need, whether or not we consciously desire them as the objects of our acquired wants. Sometimes, as in the case of our biological needs, such as hunger and thirst, our deprivation of the goods needed carries with it pains that drive us consciously to want the food and drink we need. But in the case of other natural needs, such as the need for knowledge, deprivation of the good needed does not carry with it a pain that generates a conscious want for the object of our need. The need exists whether or not we are conscious of it and actually want what we need.

Some things appear good to us *because* we want them, and they have the aspect of the good only at the time that we want them and only to the extent that we want them. In sharp contrast we ought to desire some things *because* we need them, whether we want them or not; and, *because* we need them, they are really good for us.

The two distinctions that we now have before us, distinctions generally neglected in modern thought—the distinction between natural and acquired desires, or needs and wants, and the distinction between real and merely apparent goods—enable us to state a self-evident truth that serves as the first principle of moral philosophy. *We ought to desire whatever is really good for us and nothing else.*

The criterion of self-evidence, it will be recalled, is the impossibility of thinking the opposite. It is impossible for us to think that we ought to desire what is really bad for

us, or ought not to desire what is really good for us. The very understanding of the "really good" carries with it the prescriptive note that we "ought to desire" it. We cannot understand "ought" and "really good" as related in any other way.

With this self-evident truth as a first principle, we can solve the problem posed by David Hume. By employing this first principle as a major premise and adding to it one or more descriptive truths about matters of fact (in this case, descriptive truths about human nature), we can validly reach a conclusion that is a further descriptive truth.

One example of such reasoning should suffice. Starting with the self-evident truth that we ought to desire whatever is really good for us, and adding the descriptive truth that all human beings naturally desire or need knowledge (which is tantamount to saying that knowledge is really good for us), we reach the conclusion that we ought to seek or desire knowledge. This conclusion has prescriptive truth, based on the criterion that what it prescribes conforms to right desire, desire for something that we by nature need.

The reasoning exemplified above can be carried through for all our natural desires or needs and produce a whole set of true prescriptive judgments. For the elaboration of a moral philosophy at the heart of which such reasoning lies, it is, of course, necessary to produce evidence or reasons that support an enumeration of all human needs, and also to deal with the various complications that arise with a closer examination of needs and wants. But what has been said so far suffices to solve all the problems that modern thought has posed. Failing to solve them, modern thought has denied to moral philosophy the status of genuine knowledge.

5

All real goods are not equally good. Some rank higher than others in the scale of desirables. The lesser goods are limited goods, such as sensual pleasure and wealth, things that are good only in moderation, not without limit. The greater goods are unlimited, such as knowledge, of which we cannot have too much.

But, lower or higher, all real goods are things to which we have a natural right. Our natural needs are the basis of our natural rights—rights to the things we need in order to discharge our moral obligation to seek everything that is really good for us in order to lead good human lives.

If natural needs were not the same for all human beings everywhere, at all times and under all circumstances, we would have no basis for a global doctrine that calls for the protection of human rights by all the nations of the earth.

If all goods were merely apparent, having the aspect of the good only because this or that individual happens to want them, we could not avoid the relativism and subjectivism that would reduce moral judgments to mere opinion. Having no hold on any truth about what is right and wrong, we would be left exposed to the harsh doctrine that might makes right.

Nothing more needs to be said to underline the practical importance of correcting the mistakes that reduce moral judgments to mere opinion, thereby establishing the objectivity and universality of moral values and giving moral philosophy the status of knowledge.

# PART TWO

# CHAPTER 6

# Happiness and Contentment

## 1

PEOPLE GENERALLY ESPOUSE the mistake made by most modern philosophers—that happiness is a psychological rather than an ethical state, i.e., the quality of a morally good life.

No one can legislate how the word "happiness" should be used. Unless it is used in its ethical rather than its psychological meaning, it has no significance as the ultimate end toward which we are morally obliged to strive.

Everyone, whether they make the aforementioned mistake or not, concurs in acknowledging that happiness is always an end, never a mere means. More than that, it is an ultimate or final end, sought for the sake of nothing else.

For any other good, or object of desire, we can always say that we desire it for the sake of something else. We want wealth, health, freedom, and knowledge because they

are means to some good beyond themselves. But it is impossible to complete the sentence beginning with the words "We want to be happy or want happiness *because* . . ."

Any other good that we can name is something that, obtained, leaves other goods to be sought. Each is one good among others, but happiness is not one good among others. It is the complete good, the sum of all goods, leaving nothing more to be desired. Thus conceived, happiness is not the highest good, but the total good.

What has just been said about happiness holds, though in different ways, for happiness understood as a psychological and as an ethical state. But it is much better understood when the word "happiness" is given an ethical rather than a psychological meaning. Fortunately, there is another word that aptly designates the psychological state, thus making it unnecessary to use the word "happiness" in two distinct senses.

That other word is "contentment." It cannot signify anything other than the psychological state that exists when the desires of the moment are satisfied. The more they are satisfied at a given moment, the more we regard that moment as approaching supreme contentment.

## 2

The distinctions presented in the preceding chapter (between natural and acquired desires, or needs and wants, and between real and merely apparent goods) enable us here to deal briefly with the philosophical mistake of identifying happiness with the psychological state of contentment.

If all our desires were wants, differing from individual to individual, and if all the goods that human beings desired merely appeared good to this individual or that be-

cause these individuals happened to want them, it would be impossible to avoid the conclusion that, for any individual, happiness consists in getting what he or she wanted and, getting it, enjoying contentment at that moment.

For any one individual, happiness would then be a transient and shifting thing. He might be contented one day because he had succeeded in getting the apparent goods he then wanted, but the next day might bring the frustration of his wants and with it painful discontent. Individual happiness would shift from day to day, seldom enduring for any protracted span of time. It would also differ in character from individual to individual, according to differences in their individual wants. What brings happiness to one individual might not bring happiness to another.

There are still further reasons for arguing against the identification of happiness with contentment. No one, I think, would question the moral depravity of a miser, the pathological individual who wants only to dwell in the presence of the pile of gold he has accumulated and is willing to sacrifice his health, friendships, and other real goods to do so.

If happiness is nothing but the contentment that results from satisfied wants, then the miser who has what he wants must be called happy, though by moral standards he should be regarded as a miserable creature, lacking most of the real goods that human beings need. Happiness as contentment is equally achievable by individuals who are morally good and morally bad.

Individuals come into conflict with one another in their attempts to get what they want. One individual's wanting too much wealth may result in frustrating another individual's getting the wealth he needs and also wants. An indi-

vidual who wants power over others in order to dominate and control them may interfere with the liberty that other individuals need and also want.

If a just government should do whatever it can to aid and abet the pursuit of happiness on the part of its people, that mandate cannot be carried out when happiness is identified with the contentment that results from individuals getting what they want. Confronted with conflicting wants, or with wants on the part of some that, satisfied, frustrate the satisfaction of the wants of others, no government can secure for all its citizens the conditions requisite for a successful pursuit of happiness.

With happiness conceived as contentment, its transient and shifting character, changing from day to day with changes in an individual's wants and shifting from wants that are satisfied to wants that are frustrated, makes happiness so variable and impermanent a goal that no government could possibly aid and abet the pursuit of happiness for all its people. Nor could it pledge to promote the pursuit of happiness for everyone on these terms, since the conflicting wants of different individuals would make it impossible to enable all to satisfy their wants.

All these things call for the separation of happiness from contentment. Such separation is quite possible and easy to explain once we employ the distinction between needs and wants and the distinction between real and apparent goods.

Happiness can then be defined as a whole life enriched by the cumulative possession of all the real goods that every human being needs and by the satisfaction of those individual wants that result in obtaining apparent goods that are innocuous.

The pursuit of happiness, thus conceived, consists in the

effort to discharge our moral obligation to seek whatever is really good for us and nothing else unless it is something, such as an innocuous apparent good, that does not interfere with our obtaining all the real goods we need.

A just government can then aid and abet the pursuit of happiness on the part of its people by securing their natural rights to the real goods they need—life, liberty, and whatever else an individual needs, such as the protection of health, a sufficient measure of wealth, and other real goods that individuals cannot obtain solely by their own efforts.

### 3

In spite of everything so far said, the widely prevalent error of conceiving happiness as a psychological and momentary state of contentment may still persist unless other difficulties are overcome.

For one thing, not only philosophers but also people in general find it difficult to accept a notion of happiness that makes it intrinsically unenjoyable. Conceived as the moral quality of a whole human life, happiness is strictly unenjoyable. Enjoyment occurs from moment to moment. Contentment, when it occurs, is enjoyable there and then. But at no moment in one's life can one enjoy a quality that belongs to one's life as a whole. Only when a life has been completed is it possible to say whether it has been a morally good or bad life—whether or not happiness was achieved.

Another difficulty lies in the understanding of happiness as a final end or an ultimate goal. This carries with it, both for philosophers and people in general, the notion that a final end or ultimate goal is something which, striven for,

can be reached and rested in. When happiness is conceived as contentment, it is not only something we can enjoy but also something we can cease to strive for and come to rest in—at least for a time. Not so when happiness is conceived as a whole life well lived.

It may be the final end or ultimate goal of all our striving, but it is not something we can ever cease to strive for as long as we are alive, or something we can come to rest in when achieved, because then we are no longer alive.

These difficulties can, I think, be removed by still another distinction that is generally overlooked. It is the distinction between a terminal and a normative goal. Lack of awareness of this distinction led John Dewey, in his *Human Nature and Conduct,* to deny that there are any final ends in this life. Everything we seek, according to Dewey, is a means to some good beyond itself. None is, therefore, a final end or ultimate goal, not even happiness conceived as contentment. Enjoying it one day or for a short span of time leaves more to be striven for in what remains of one's life.

To make the difference between a terminal and a normative goal clear, examples of them should suffice.

You plan a trip to Vienna. You make decisions about the means of getting there, and you take the steps to put those decisions into action. You finally arrive in Vienna—the termination of your trip—and, for some period of time, you are at rest so far as your travels are concerned. In this simple instance of aiming at an end and taking the means to achieve it, Vienna is a terminal goal. Reaching it and resting in it is an enjoyable experience.

The conductor of a symphony orchestra prepares to play a certain musical composition at a concert some time ahead.

He studies the piece of music. He rehearses the orchestra a number of times. Finally, the day of the concert arrives and the conductor puts all this prior work into effect by doing his best to lead the orchestra in a rendition of the composition that achieves a high degree of musical excellence.

Let us suppose the conductor succeeds. The musical excellence he has aimed at and achieved is a normative rather than a terminal goal. It does not exist at any moment during the playing of the composition. The conductor and the orchestra never reach it, in the sense of being able to rest in it, because the excellence aimed at comes into existence temporally. It has its being only in the whole span of time that it took to play the piece.

Normative goals are goals that exist only in temporal wholes, not from moment to moment or at any one moment. What is true of the normative goal that is aimed at in the rendition of a piece of music is similarly true of the excellence aimed at in the production of a dramatic work on the stage, in the production of a ballet, in any of the performing arts, and, as well, in the playing of athletic games that run for a period of time.

How different is the excellence aimed at by architects and builders who, when they have completed their work, can point to a fine edifice in existence as the result. The building completed is a terminal goal which can be reached, rested in, and enjoyed at a given moment.

One cannot say the building the architect is working on is a good building until it is completed and stands there to be admired. So, too, one cannot say of a football or baseball game that it is a good game until the last play has been made and the whistle blows. When, at a baseball game, fans

stand up in the seventh inning to stretch, one may say to the other, "It's a good game, isn't it?" The other should reply, "No, it's not over yet; it's becoming a good game; if it's as well played in the remaining innings as it has been played so far, it will have been a good game when it's finished."

Trite though it may be to say so, leading a morally good life or living well resembles the conduct of any of the performing arts or the playing of athletic games. The happiness which is identical with a morally good life is a normative goal. The excellence aimed at inheres in a temporal whole—a life from birth to death.

If an individual at some midpoint in life is asked whether or not he has achieved happiness, the answer should be like that given by the baseball fan: "No, not yet, my life is not over; but if its closing years continue to have the same quality as the years gone by, I dare to say that I will have led a happy life when it has come to an end."

What is true of terminal goals is equally true of normative goals. The goal aimed at controls one's decision about the means to be taken to achieve it. The fact that a terminal goal can be reached and rested in, while a normative goal cannot be, makes no difference to the point. A normative goal aimed at, no less than a terminal goal, determines what we must do to achieve it.

Thus there should be no difficulty in understanding how happiness as the excellence of a whole life well lived, a morally good life, functions as a final end that is a normative not a terminal goal. Every step we take in that direction brings us nearer to its full realization, even though we never enjoy that full realization at any one moment. Every means we choose is good or bad accordingly as it tends in

the right or the wrong direction—toward or away from the final end we are aiming at. Great insight is to be found in the statement that rightly directed means *are* the end aimed at in the process of becoming achieved or realized.

One further point should be noted. When, according to John Dewey, there are no final ends and every end is a means to something beyond itself, we are under no inexorable moral obligation to aim at any one of these ends. We may acknowledge a hypothetical imperative of the following sort: *if* we wish to achieve this particular end, *then* we ought to choose such and such means to achieve it.

The understanding of the "if" and "then" indicates the hypothetical character of the imperative—the prescriptive judgment. Only when the end aimed at is truly a final end (and it can be that in this life only if it is also a normative rather than a terminal end) must we acknowledge a categorical rather than a hypothetical imperative.

The self-evident principle that we ought to seek everything that is really good for us puts us under a moral obligation that is categorical. There are no "ifs" and "thens" about it. We cannot say "If we wish to lead a morally good life, then . . ." We are under a categorical obligation to try to do so.

I said a moment ago that happiness can be a final end *in this life* only if it is a normative rather than a terminal goal. I repeat that here to call attention to the fact that, in Christian moral theology, what holds for terrestrial, temporal happiness does not hold for heavenly, eternal happiness—the happiness of those who, in the presence of God, enjoy the beatific vision. The latter is a terminal goal, as the former is not.

4

Still another mistake about happiness is to be found in John Stuart Mill's *Utilitarianism*. He vacillates between identifying, in certain passages, happiness with momentary contentment, and, in other passages, conceiving it as truly a final end, the excellence to be desired in a whole human life. His failure to distinguish between real and apparent goods as the objects of natural and acquired desires (needs and wants) adds to the confusion. But that is not the mistake to which I now wish to call attention.

Rather, this mistake consists in his setting before us two ends, each of which is supposedly a final or ultimate goal, yet one of which is to be subordinated to the other. On the one hand, Mill proposes as a self-evident truth that his own happiness is the ultimate goal at which the individual should aim. On the other hand, he also proposes that each of us should work for what he calls "the general happiness," sometimes also referred to as the greatest good of the greatest number.

When there is any conflict between these two aims, the latter should take precedence over the former. We should aim at the general happiness even if that does not also serve the purpose of procuring for ourselves our own individual happiness.

It is impossible for there to be two ultimate goals that are not ordered to one another; and if they are so ordered by the subordination of the one to the other, then both cannot be ultimate goals.

The mistake on Mill's part might have been avoided if he had known and understood the distinction between the *bonum commune hominis* (the happiness or ultimate good that is the same for or common to all human beings) and the

*bonum commune communitatis* (the common good of the organized community in which its members participate).

Because each human being as a person is an end to be served, not a means to be used, the organized community, in relation to its members, is a means, not an end. The happiness of the individual person is the one and only ultimate goal or final end in this life. It is a common good in the sense that it is the same for all human beings.

The good that is common to and shared by all human beings as members of society (the *bonum commune communitatis*) is an end to be served by the organized community as a whole. We sometimes refer to this common good as the general welfare. Participating in the common good or general welfare provides the members of society with means that serve the pursuit of their individual happiness. By aiming directly at the common good or general welfare, a good society and a just government also aim indirectly at the happiness of all the persons who constitute the society and are under its government.

The common good or general welfare is only the proximate goal at which a good society and a just government should aim. The goal achieved serves as a means to society's ultimate goal—the individual happiness of each of society's members or the general happiness of all.

The crucial point here is that individuals by themselves cannot work *directly* for the general happiness—the happiness of all other persons in the society in which they live. They can do so *indirectly* only by working with others for the common good or general welfare of the political community, which is itself a means to the happiness of each and every individual.

5

Finally, we come to a mistake about happiness to be found in Kant's moral philosophy. What I have in mind here is not the mistake that is prevalent throughout much of modern thought—the mistake of identifying happiness with the contentment experienced when our desires, whatever they may be, are satisfied.

Kant does make that mistake and, as a result of it, rejects any moral philosophy that regards happiness as an ultimate end, for which means should be chosen, as merely utilitarian and pragmatic. In this connection he writes contemptuously of "the serpentine windings of utilitarianism." He dismisses any utilitarian or pragmatic ethics, which is concerned with means and ends, as devoid of what is essential to a sound moral philosophy, namely moral duties, obligations that are categorical, not hypothetical.

As we have already seen, his charge against a moral philosophy that makes happiness, properly conceived, an ultimate goal is without foundation. It may apply to happiness when that is identified with contentment, but it does not apply to happiness conceived as a morally good life—a normative, not a terminal, goal. We are under a categorical imperative to aim at the excellence of a morally good life when we acknowledge the self-evident truth that we ought to seek everything that is really good for us.

If we drop the word "happiness" and deal instead with a morally good life, we can pinpoint the error that is so dominant in Kant's moral philosophy. It is a mistake also to be found in antiquity (in Platonic thought and in the teachings of the Stoics), as well as in the writings of other modern philosophers.

It consists in saying, as Kant so explicitly does say, that

a good or righteous will, by discharging its moral obligations, suffices for the purpose of leading a morally good life.
Plato's way of saying the same thing is to be found in the
*Apology* where, at the end, he has Socrates declare that "no
harm can come to a good man in this life or the next." Ep-
ictetus and other Roman Stoics repeat again and again that
a good will suffices for the achievement of happiness.

The error here resides in the word "suffices." There can
be no question at all that having moral virtue (which is
identical with having a will rightly directed to happiness as
the ultimate goal and habitually disposed to choose the right
means for achieving it) is absolutely necessary for the leading of a morally good life. Necessary, yes, but not by itself
sufficient. The other, equally necessary but also not sufficient, ingredient is being blessed by good fortune.

There are many real goods, most of them external goods,
such as wealth, a healthy environment, political liberty, and
so on, that are not wholly within the power of the most
virtuous individual to obtain for himself or herself. Obtaining these goods in the pursuit of happiness depends on
fortunate circumstances that are beyond the individual's
power to control.

Deprived of these goods of fortune, a human life can be
ruined even for the most morally virtuous individual. He
or she may be a morally good person and still be deprived
of the happiness of a life well lived by such misfortunes as
enslavement, grinding poverty, crippling illness, the loss of
friends and loved ones. Being a morally good human being
does not automatically result in the achievement of a morally good life.

Aristotle sums up this critical point in his single sentence definition of happiness as "a whole life, lived in ac-

cordance with moral virtue, and accompanied by a moderate possession of wealth" [and all other external goods that are ours through the blessings of good fortune]. I have put in brackets what I think serves to explicate a point too briefly expressed.

Were this not so, there would be little or no reason for all the historic efforts that have been made to reform our political and economic institutions by removing injustices and improving the conditions under which human beings live. If happiness can be achieved by moral virtue alone, then why abolish slavery, why attempt to alleviate grinding poverty or destitution, why be concerned with providing health care and the protection of health, why extend the suffrage to all so that all human beings can exercise political liberty by having a voice in their own government?

To these questions, there can be only one answer. The political and economic reforms that have occurred in the course of history would be pointless if moral virtue by itself sufficed for the attainment of happiness and the leading of a good life. Nothing more need be said, in my judgment, to persuade anyone of the seriousness of the mistake made by Plato, by the Stoics, by Immanuel Kant, and by other modern philosophers.

# CHAPTER 7
# Freedom of Choice

## 1

WHEN PEOPLE THINK of freedom what they tend to have in mind is a freedom the existence of which cannot be and has never been denied. It is also a freedom that everyone possesses and of which no one can be completely deprived.

It is the freedom we possess when we are able to do as we please or wish. We possess it to the highest degree under the most favorable circumstances: the absence of coercion, restraint, duress, and the presence of enabling means. Such obstacles as coercion and duress limit the extent to which we can do as we please; so does the lack of enabling means. As R. H. Tawney said, the poor man is not free to dine at the Ritz.

However, no one, not even the slave in chains or the prisoner in solitary confinement, is totally devoid of the

freedom to do as he wishes. There are still some respects, however slight, in which he can do as he pleases.

Another circumstantial freedom is political liberty. It is a freedom possessed by those who are fortunate enough to live in a republic, under constitutional government, and who have been enfranchised as citizens with suffrage—with a voice in their own government. That such freedom exists cannot be denied, for at least some human beings if not for all; but some voices have been raised against its being desirable for or deserved by all.

The two remaining types of freedom do not depend upon outer circumstances, and both have been the subject of controversies in which their existence has been denied.

One of these is the acquired freedom of being able to will as one ought. Only through acquired moral virtue and practical wisdom does anyone come to possess such freedom. It is a freedom from the passions and the sensuous desires that lead us to do what we ought not to do, or not to do what we ought to do. When, in the conflict between reason and the passions, reason dominates, then we are able to will as we ought in conformity to the moral law, or to normative rules of conduct.

Obviously, those who deny that there are any objective moral values, any valid oughts or normative prescriptions, cannot help but deny existence to the moral freedom thus described. Even those who affirm its existence do not regard it as having universality. Whereas the circumstantial freedom of being able to do as one wishes is possessed to some degree by everyone, even those under the most unfavorable circumstances, individuals either have moral freedom or lack it entirely; they either have or have not

acquired the moral virtue and practical wisdom on which it depends.

We are left, finally, with a fourth type of freedom that has been the subject of the most extended and intricate controversy over the centuries. Its existence has been affirmed by a large number of philosophers and denied by an equally large number, most of them modern, and also by a host of modern scientists.

For those who affirm its existence, it is universally possessed because it is regarded by them as inherent in human nature: it is a natural freedom, neither affected by circumstances nor dependent on acquired developments.

This natural freedom is the freedom of the will in its acts of choice. Freedom of choice consists in always being able to choose otherwise, no matter what one has chosen in any particular instance. As contrasted with a freedom that consists in being able to do as one wishes, it might be described as freedom to will as one wishes.

When we declare that freedom is a natural human right we must have in mind the two circumstantial freedoms—the freedom to do as one pleases (within the circumscription of just laws) and the political liberty that comes with citizenship and suffrage. There is no meaning to the statement that one has a right to moral liberty, which can be possessed only with acquired virtue and wisdom; or a right to freedom of choice which, if it exists, is a natural endowment possessed by all.

However, unless freedom of choice does exist, it is difficult to understand the basis of our right to these other freedoms. If we do not have freedom of choice, what reason can be given for our right to do as we please or to exercise a voice in our own government?

These considerations, and there are others to which we will subsequently come, make the controversy about the existence of freedom of choice one with far-reaching consequences.

## 2

This chapter differs from all its predecessors. In them we dealt with mistaken philosophical views the errors or inadequacies of which could be pointed out and corrected. That cannot be done here.

With knowledge of all the ins and outs of the controversy, I cannot show that the exponents of free choice are right and that the determinists who oppose free choice are wrong. The philosophical defect here is not so much a demonstrable philosophical error as a manifest misunderstanding of the issue itself.

That misunderstanding lies mainly on the side of the modern philosophers and scientists who are determinists. What I am saying here is not that their denial of freedom of choice is a demonstrable mistake, but rather that they do not correctly understand what they have denied—the premises upon which an affirmation of freedom of choice rests.

Prior to the end of the nineteenth century, determinists held that all the phenomena of nature are governed by causal laws through the operation of which effects are necessitated by their causes. Nothing happens by chance, in that sense of the term which regards a chance event as something uncaused. In their view, an intrinsically unpredictable free choice is exactly like a chance event and so cannot occur within the natural domain. While it is true that a free choice and a chance event are both unpredictable with cer-

titude and precision, it is not true that both are uncaused.

Beginning at the end of the nineteenth century and becoming more significant in our own time, science added statistical laws or probabilistic formulations to causal laws, and in doing so introduced aspects of indeterminacy into the realm of natural phenomena.

Such indeterminacy, however, does not reduce to the causelessness of chance. A handful of philosophers and Nobel Prize winning scientists advanced the supposition that such interdeterminacy might make room for freedom of choice within the bounds of nature; but more sober minds rightly dismissed the supposition. The causal indeterminacy involved in certain scientific formulations, especially those of quantum mechanics, simply bears no resemblance to the causal indeterminacy involved in freedom of choice.

What the determinists who deny freedom of choice on the grounds stated above fail to understand is that the exponents of free choice place the action of the will outside the domain of the physical phenomena studied by science. If their theory of freedom of choice conceived it as a physical event in the same way that the action of our senses and the motion of our passions are physical events, then they would have to accept the arguments of the determinists as adequate grounds for denying free choice.

But that is not the case. The will, as they conceive it, is an intellectual, not a sensuous, appetite or faculty of desire and decision. In their view, the human mind, consisting of both intellect and will, is to be sharply distinguished from the senses, the memory, the imagination, and the passions. The latter may operate according to the same principles and laws that govern all the other phenomena of the physical world, but the intellect and the will, being immaterial, do

not act in accordance with these principles and laws. They are governed by laws of their own.

The acts of the intellect are either necessitated or they are arbitrary. They are necessitated when they are acts of genuine knowledge, for the intellect cannot say no to a self-evident truth, nor can it say no to any proposition that is supported by evidence and reasons that put it beyond a reasonable doubt or give it predominance over all contrary opinions.

In the above cases, all the intellect's judgments are necessitated. Only when it is confronted with mere opinions, unsupported by evidence and reasons, is its judgment arbitrary—an act of the intellect moved by a free choice on the part of the will rather than an act of the intellect moved by the truth laid before it. In neither case is the action of the intellect uncaused or a chance event.

Like the acts of the intellect, some acts of the will are necessitated and some involve freedom of choice. The only object that necessitates the will is the complete or total good. In the presence of the complete or total good, it cannot turn away from it and will anything else. Thus, when happiness is understood to be the *totum bonum*—the sum of all real goods—it attracts the will with necessity. We cannot will not to seek happiness. Our willing happiness as our ultimate end is not an uncaused act.

All other goods are partial goods. Each one is one good among others. In the presence of such goods as objects of desire, the will is not necessitated, which is another way of saying that its choice of one rather than another partial good is a free choice on its part. Such indeterminacy on the part of the will is utterly different from the causal indeterminacy to be found in quantum mechanics. But in both cases,

the causal indeterminacy does not reduce to chance—the complete negation of causality.

The theories of the freedom of the will and of freedom of choice are many and complicated. I do not pretend that the foregoing briefly stated points do justice to their variety and complexity. However, I do claim that, in all of them, the affirmation of freedom of choice rests on the points made—the immateriality of the will; the difference between the way its acts are caused and the operation of causes in the realm of physical phenomena; and above all the insistence that the causal indeterminacy of the will does not reduce a free choice to a chance event.*

What happens by chance, according to the determinists, is totally unpredictable; and since, according to them, nothing is totally unpredictable, nothing happens by chance. While the causally indeterminate events in the realm of quantum phenomena and the causally indeterminate acts of free choice are both intrinsically unpredictable (in the sense of not being predictable with the certitude appropriate to the necessitation of effects by their causes), they are not totally unpredictable. Prediction is possible in both cases with varying degrees of probability. The possibility of probable predictions dismisses the identification of such causal indeterminacy with chance.

The determinists' misunderstanding of what is involved in freedom of choice makes the historical controversy about this subject an illusory one. The issues are not joined.

*The Institute for Philosophical Research published, after eight years of work, two volumes of *The Idea of Freedom*, in 1958 and 1961. In the second of those volumes over three hundred pages (223–525) were devoted to delineating and clarifying the controversy between the determinists and the exponents of free will and freedom of choice. Readers who wish to go beyond the brief and inadequate summary here given are referred to those pages.

The determinists do not argue against the truth of the premises on which the affirmation of free choice rests, but reject free choice as something that it is not (i.e., a chance happening) and as something that, if not chance, cannot occur within the domain of physical phenomena, which they regard as exhaustive of the real world.

The exponents of free choice do not argue for the premises on which their affirmation of free choice rests. They do not successfully attempt to show that the domain of physical phenomena is not the whole of reality or how the causality that operates in the realm of immaterial phenomena differs from the causality that operates in the physical world. The only thing they are sufficiently clear about, and rightly insistent on, is that freedom of choice as they conceive it is not to be identified with chance. And this is the one thing that the determinists stubbornly ignore.

Though both sides fail to come to grips with one another, the main failure of understanding is on the side of the determinists.

### 3

The controversy between the determinists and the exponents of freedom of choice goes beyond the denial and affirmation of that freedom. It concerns such questions as whether moral responsibility, praise and blame, the justice of rewards and punishments, depend on man's having freedom of choice.

David Hume was certainly correct when, having first identified a free choice with mere chance, he concluded that moral responsibility was incompatible with free choice. What a person does by chance, he cannot be held responsible for, praised or blamed for, rewarded or punished for. Hume's

error, of course, was in the identification of free choice with chance.

The determinists in recent times have divided into two groups—the soft-determinists and the hard-determinists. The soft-determinists hold the view that the circumstantial freedom of being able to do as one pleases provides sufficient grounds for attributing moral responsibility to those who act with such freedom. They can be praised and blamed, rewarded and punished, for what they do, even though what they do was not freely chosen on their part, because they could not have chosen otherwise.

They were determined by their entire past, by everything that entered into the constitution of themselves, to act as they did. However, their action, proceeding from themselves as thus constituted, was *their* action and so they can be held responsible for it.

The hard-determinists disagree. While denying freedom of choice, they concede that, without it, no one should be held morally responsible for what they do; no one should be praised or blamed, rewarded or punished.

As against the soft-determinists, the exponents of freedom of choice maintain that such freedom is indispensable to every aspect of the moral life. How can anyone be held responsible for an act that he could not avoid having chosen to perform—that was a product of the factors in his present makeup deriving from his whole past? Why should the individual be praised or blamed, rewarded or punished, for acts not freely chosen, acts that might have been different had he chosen otherwise?

The punishment for criminal actions may have some pragmatic or utilitarian justification. It may serve the purpose of reforming the criminal and of deterring others from

committing the same crime, thus protecting society in the future from such depredations. But how can punishment be retributively just if the criminal was not morally responsible for what he did because it was not a free choice on his part?

On these counts, in my judgment, the position taken by the exponents of free choice is sounder than the position taken by the soft-determinists. There are still other considerations in its favor.

One turns on the resolution of the issue between those who regard moral values and prescriptive judgments as matters of mere opinion and those who regard moral philosophy as genuine knowledge. If the latter view prevails, moral virtue—the habitual direction of the will to the right end and the habitual disposition of the will to choose the right means for achieving that end—is an indispensable (a necessary, but not sufficient) ingredient in the pursuit of happiness.

What merit would attach to moral virtue if the acts that form such habitual tendencies and dispositions were not acts of free choice on the part of the individual who was in the process of acquiring moral virtue? Persons of vicious moral character would have their characters formed in a manner no different from the way in which the character of a morally virtuous person was formed—by acts entirely determined, and that could not have been otherwise by freedom of choice.

The other consideration concerns controversies in science and philosophy—controversies over serious issues about what is true and false, or more and less true. What do these controversies amount to if they cannot be settled or resolved by the appeal to better evidence and better reasons?

Certainly they cannot be thus settled if the better evidence and better reasons do not necessitate the intellects of the parties to the issue. Such necessitation is different from the causal determination of a scientific or philosophical judgment by factors operating out of the past of the scientist or philosopher.

# CHAPTER 8

# Human Nature

## 1

IT IS NOW GENERALLY ACCEPTED that the species *Homo sapiens* is older than we once thought, having emerged within the hominid family perhaps as long ago as 35,000 to 50,000 years. It is also generally agreed that all human beings alive today, and all that have been alive since *Homo sapiens* first appeared on earth, are members of one and the same species.

Nevertheless, in the twentieth century, the essential sameness of all human beings, by virtue of their participating in the same specific nature, has been widely challenged. The challenge has come from cultural anthropologists, from sociologists, from other behavioral scientists, and even from historians.

That challenge, tantamount to a denial of human nature, is rooted in a profound mistake, but one that is not, in origin at least, a philosophical mistake. However, it

should be added that philosophers have not been at pains to correct the error and that it has become for some philosophers—the existentialists—the root error in their thought. Merleau-Ponty, for example, has declared that "it is the nature of man not to have a nature."

I said a moment ago that the denial of human nature is a profound mistake—one with extremely serious consequences for philosophy, especially moral philosophy. To have some sense of this we need only look back to Chapter 5 on moral values. There we saw that the distinction between acquired and natural desires—the needs inherent in human nature—led to the distinction between apparent and real goods, and that in turned helped to establish the truth of prescriptive judgments and laid the basis for our understanding of natural rights, human rights.

If moral philosophy is to have a sound factual basis, it is to be found in the facts about human nature and nowhere else. If that basis is denied us by a denial of human nature, the only other alternative lies in the extreme rationalism of Immanuel Kant, which proceeds without any consideration of the facts of human life and with no concern for the variety of cases to which moral prescriptions must be applied in a manner that is flexible rather than rigorous.

At this point readers may call for a pause and an explanation. What can possibly be meant by the denial of human nature? We are all human beings, are we not? It must be extremely rare, if it ever happened at all, that anyone would have some doubt about whether a specimen being examined was human or not.

This being so, do not the criteria we employ to determine whether we are dealing with a human being imply some understanding on our part of the common traits be-

longing to all members of the human species? These common traits constitute the nature that is the same in all members of the species. That is what we mean by human nature, is it not?

## 2

Let me now try to explain what it is that leads to a denial of human nature.

First, consider other animal species. If you were to investigate any one of them as carefully as possible, you would find that the members of the same species, living in their natural habitats, manifest a remarkable degree of similarity. You might find differences in size, weight, shape, or coloration among the individuals you examined. You might even find deviations here and there from what would have become evident as the normal behavior of that species. But, by and large, you would be impressed by the similitudes that reigned in the populations you examined.

The dominant likeness of all members of the species would lead you to dismiss as relatively insignificant the differences you found, most of which can be explained as the result of slightly different environmental conditions. That dominant likeness would constitute the nature of the species in question.

Now consider the human species. It inhabits the globe. Its members live in all the hemispheres and regions, under the most widely divergent environmental conditions. Let us suppose you were to take the time to visit human populations wherever they existed—all of them. Let the visit not be a casual one, but one in which you lived for a time with each of these populations and studied them closely.

You would come away with the very opposite impres-

sion from the one you took away from your investigation of the populations that belonged to one or another animal species. You were there impressed by the overwhelming similitude that reigned among its members. Here, however, you would find that the differences were dominant rather than the similarities.

Of course human beings, like other animals, must eat, drink, and sleep. They all have certain biological traits in common. There can be no doubt that they have the nature of animals. But when you come to their human traits, how different one human population will be from another.

They will differ in the languages they speak, and you will have some difficulty in making an accurate count of the vast number of different languages you will have found.

They will differ in their dress, in their adornments, in their cuisines, in their customs and manners, in the organization of their families, in the institutions of their societies, in their beliefs, in their standards of conduct, in the turn of their minds, in almost everything that enters into the ways of life they lead. These differences will be so multitudinous and variegated that you might, unless cautioned against doing so, tend to be persuaded that they were not all members of the same species.

In any case, you cannot avoid being persuaded that, in the human case, membership in the same species does not carry with it the dominant similitude that you would find in the case of other animal species. On the contrary, the differences between one human race and another, between one racial variety and another, between one ethnic group and another, between one nation and another, would seem to be dominant.

It is this that might lead you to the conclusion that there

is no human nature in the sense in which a certain constant nature can be attributed to other species of animals. Even if you did not reach that conclusion yourself, you might understand how that conclusion is plausible.

Unlike most other species of animals, the members of the human species appear to have formed subgroups that differentiated themselves, one from another. Each subgroup has a distinctive character. The differences that separate one subgroup from another are so numerous and so profound that they defy you to say what remains, if anything, that might be regarded as a human nature common to all.

Let me be sure it is understood that the denial of human nature rests ultimately on the striking contrast between the dominant similitude that prevails among the members of other animal species and the apparently dominant differentiation that prevails among the subgroups of the human species. If a specific nature is a nature common to members of the species, then other animal species would clearly have specific natures, each its own. But the human species does not seem to have a specific nature like that.

Even if we admit, as we must, that all members of the human species do have certain traits in common, mainly the biological attributes or characteristics that they share with other of the higher animals, these seem subordinate to all the behavioral differences that separate one human subgroup from another. Far from sharing the same behavioral attributes or characteristics, such groups are differentiated from one another in these respects.


3

Looked at one way, the denial of human nature is correct. The members of the human species do not have a specific

or common nature *in the same sense* that the members of other animal species do. This, by the way, is one of the most remarkable differences between man and other animals, one that tends to corroborate the conclusion that man differs from other animals in kind, not in degree.

But to concede that the members of the human species do not have a specific or common nature *in the same sense* that the members of other animal species do is not to admit that they have *no specific nature whatsoever*. An alternative remains open; namely, that the members of the human species all have the same nature in a quite different sense.

In what sense then is there a human nature, a specific nature that is common to all members of the species? The answer can be given in a single word: *potentialities*. Human nature is constituted by all the potentialities that are the species-specific properties common to all members of the human species.

It is the essence of a potentiality to be capable of a wide variety of different actualizations. Thus, for example, the human potentiality for syntactical speech is actualized in thousands of different human languages. Having that potentiality, a human infant placed at the moment of birth in one or another human subgroup, each with its own language, would learn to speak that language. The differences among all human languages are superficial as compared with the potentiality for learning and speaking any human language that is present in all human infants at birth.

What has just been said about one human potentiality applies to all the others that are the common, specific traits of the human being. Each underlies all the differences that arise among human subgroups as a result of the many dif-

ferent ways in which the same potentiality can be actualized. To recognize this is tantamount to acknowledging the superficiality of the differences that separate one human subgroup from another, as compared with the samenesses that unite all human beings as members of the same species and as having the same specific nature.

In other species of animals, the samenesses that unite the members and constitute their common nature are not potentialities but rather quite determinate characteristics, behavioral as well as anatomical and physiological. This accounts for the impression derived from studying these other species—the impression of a dominant similitude among its members.

Turning to the human species, the opposite impression of dominant differences among subgroups can also be accounted for. The explanation of it lies in the fact that, as far as behavioral characteristics are concerned, the common nature all the subgroups share consists entirely of species-specific potentialities. These are actualized by these subgroups in all the different ways that we find when we make a global study of mankind.

A newcomer to the behavioral sciences, sociobiology, has tried to show that to a significant extent animal and human behavior is genetically determined. So far as the human species is concerned, what little truth there is in sociobiology applies only to the genetic determination of human potentialities, not to their behavioral development.

The mistake that the cultural anthropologists, the sociologists, and other behavioral scientists make when they deny the existence of human nature has its root in their failure to understand that the specific nature in the case of the human species is radically different from the specific

nature in the case of other animal species.

Let me repeat once more what that difference is. In the case of other animal species, the specific nature common to all members of the species is constituted mainly by quite determinate characteristics or attributes. In the case of the human species, it is constituted by determinable, not wholly determinate, characteristics or attributes. An innate potentiality is precisely that—something determinable, not wholly determinate, and determinable in a wide variety of ways.

Man is to a great extent a self-made creature. Given a range of potentialities at birth, he makes himself what he becomes by how he freely chooses to develop those potentialities by the habits he forms.

It is thus that differentiated subgroups of human beings came into existence. Once in existence, they subsequently affected the way in which those born into these subgroups came to develop the acquired characteristics that differentiate one subgroup from another. These acquired characteristics, especially the behavioral ones, are the results of acculturation; or, even more generally, results of the way in which those born into this or that subgroup are nurtured differently.

No other animal is a self-made creature in the sense indicated above. On the contrary, other animals have determinate natures, natures genetically determined in such a way that they do not admit of a wide variety of different developments as they mature.

Human nature is also genetically determined; but, because the genetic determination consists, behaviorally, in an innate endowment of potentialities that are determinable in different ways, human beings differ remarkably from one another as they mature.

However they originated in the first place, most of those differences are due to differences in acculturation, to nurtural differences. To confuse nature with nurture is a philosophical mistake of the first order. That philosophical mistake underlies the denial of human nature. Contemporary philosophers should have pointed it out to their academic colleagues in the fields of behavioral science. The persistence of the denial would seem to indicate that they failed to do so.

4

The correction of the philosophical mistake just mentioned is of the greatest importance because of the consequences that follow from doing so.

Most important of all is overcoming the persistent prejudice—the racist, sexist, elitist, even ethnic prejudice—that one portion or subgroup of mankind is distinctly inferior by nature to another. The inferiority may exist, but it is not an inferiority due to nature, but to nurture.

When, for most of the centuries of recorded history, the female half of the population was nurtured—reared and treated—as inferior to the male half, that nurturing made them apparently inferior when they matured. To have correctly attributed that apparent inferiority to their nurturing would have instantly indicated how it could be eliminated. But when it is incorrectly attributed to their nature at birth, it is accepted as irremediable.

What I have said about the sexist prejudice concerning the inequality of men and women applies to all the racist and ethnic prejudices about human inequality that still exist among mankind. All these apparent inequalities are

nurtural. None is a natural inequality between one human subgroup and another.

In the centuries prior to this one, the elitist view taken by the propertied class about the inferiority of the working class was similarly grounded in grave deficiencies in the nurturing of workers who went to work at an early age without schooling and who often toiled fourteen hours a day and seven days a week.

Thomas Jefferson was right in declaring that all human beings are created (or, if you will, are by nature) equal. They are also, in terms of their individual differences, unequal in the varying degrees to which they possess the species-specific potentialities common to all.

These individual inequalities, when they are recognized as subordinate to the basic equality of all human beings in their common humanity or specific nature, do not generate difficulties that must be overcome or eradicated in order to increase social justice. But when inequalities between human subgroups that are entirely due to nurture are taken for natural inequalities, that mistake must be overcome and eradicated for the sake of social justice.

The correction of the mistake that confuses nature with nurture leads to certain conclusions that many readers may find disconcerting. All the cultural and nurtural differences that separate one human subgroup from another are superficial as compared with the underlying common human nature that unites the members of mankind.

Although our samenesses are more important than our differences, we have an inveterate tendency to stress the differences that divide us rather than the samenesses that unite us. We find it difficult to believe that the human mind

is the same everywhere because we fail to realize that all the differences, however striking, between the mind of Western man and the mind of human beings nurtured in the various Eastern cultures are, in the last analysis, superficial—entirely the result of different nurturing.

If a world cultural community is ever to come into existence, it will retain cultural pluralism or diversity with respect to all matters that are accidental in human life— such things as cuisine, dress, manners, customs, and the like. These are the things that vary from one human subgroup to another according as these subgroups differ in the way they nurture their members.

In contrast, the common elements that will unite all human beings in a single, cultural community will be related to such essentials as truth in science and philosophy, moral values and human rights, man's understanding of himself, and the wisdom that is the highest good of the human mind. When that happens, we will have at last overcome the nurtural illusion that there is a Western mind and an Eastern mind, a European mind and an African mind, or a civilized mind and a primitive mind. There is only a human mind and it is one and the same in all human beings.

# CHAPTER 9
# Human Society

## 1

ONE OF MAN'S inherent potentialities and, therefore, innate propensities, is to associate with his fellows. He is by nature a social animal and needs to live in society.

Another inherent potentiality is the capacity for engaging in government, and this, too, gives rise to an innate tendency and a natural need.

Other animals are gregarious, forming elaborate societies, as do the social insects (bees, wasps, ants, termites), or herding together in one way or another, as do wolves in packs and fish in schools. Man differs from them in two respects. One is the way in which members of the human species form societies. The other lies in the fact that man, of all the social animals, is the only political animal: a law-making animal, one that forms a civil society, a state or political community, and establishes political institutions.

There is still one further striking difference between the social life of the human species and of other gregarious animals. Human beings live together and associate with one another in a variety of ways: they live in families; they live in tribal or village communities; they live in states or civil societies; and, in addition to all these, they associate in numerous organized subgroups to serve one purpose or another. Nothing like this variety of modes of association exists in any other species of gregarious animal.

To say that man's gregarious behavior is exactly like that of the other social animals, controlled by the same factors and operating in the same way, would appear to fly in the face of the most obvious facts. Nevertheless, we cannot avoid facing the problem that arises from acknowledging the fact that only some animals are by nature gregarious or social.

What is common to man and to other social animals is that they are *naturally* gregarious—the propensity to associate is ingrained in them at birth. But are they naturally gregarious in the same sense of that word "naturally"?

If one concentrates for a moment on the elaborately organized hives, colonies, or mounds of the social insects, one finds that the mode or plan of organization is exactly the same for the insects of a given species, generation after generation, for as long as that species endures. The way in which the members of that particular species of insect associate with one another, the structure of their social organization, the pattern of their social behavior, is genetically determined by instincts with which that particular species is endowed.

What is so obviously true of the social insects is equally, though perhaps not so obviously, true of the social groupings and behavior of the gregarious higher animals. Their

gregariousness is natural in the sense of being genetically determined for each generation of a particular species as long as that species endures.

We have already noted, in the preceding chapter, that in sharp contrast to all other animal species, the members of the human species divide into a multitude of subgroups characterized by the widest variety of distinctive traits or attributes. It is this fact that led to doubts and denials about the existence of a human nature common to all.

The same type of fact raises a question about the naturalness of human societies. Wherever on this globe one finds human beings living in families, in tribal organizations, and in civil societies or states, those domestic societies, those tribes or villages, and those civil societies or states are structured, organized, and operated in the widest variety of different ways.

They can, therefore, hardly be genetically determined by instinctive endowments. Were that the case they would all have to be the same, since whatever is an instinctive endowment is present in exactly the same way in every member of a given species.

If human societies are not natural in origin, how then do they come into being? The answer that is usually given is: *by convention;* or, in other words, by the voluntary agreement of individuals to form an association for this purpose or that. This is certainly the way that many associations are formed—clubs, hospitals, universities, business or professional associations, companies, corporations, and so on. They are all voluntarily instituted, set up and organized by conventions entered into by the associating parties.

Nevertheless, in antiquity and in the Middle Ages the

three main forms of human association—the family, the tribe or village, and civil society or the state—were all regarded as natural. Only in modern times, beginning with *The Leviathan* of Thomas Hobbes and culminating in *The Social Contract* of Jean-Jacques Rousseau, has civil society or the state been declared to be wholly conventional, not in any sense natural as might be the human family and as are the associations formed by other gregarious animals.

## 2

The most important of the modern philosophical mistakes about society is to be found in the theory of the social contract as the conventional origin of the state or civil society. It rests on two myths.

One is the myth that goes by the name of "the state of nature." This phrase, when used by Hobbes, Locke, or Rousseau in their slightly varying accounts of the origin of civil society, signifies a condition of human life on earth in which individuals live in isolation from one another and live anarchically with complete autonomy.

What is called a "state of nature" is utterly mythical and never existed on earth. This should be manifest to everyone in the light of the incontrovertible fact that the human species could not have survived without the existence of families for the preservation of infants unable to take care of themselves.

The second myth, inseparable from the first, is the fiction that human beings, dissatisfied with the precariousness and brutality of living in a state of nature, decided to put up with it no longer and to agree upon certain conventions and rules for living together under some form of gov-

ernment that replaced anarchy and eliminated their isolation and autonomy.

Of the three modern exponents of this social contract theory, Rousseau at least concedes that the social contract and the state of nature have no historical reality, but only constitute a hypothesis to explain how civil society came into existence. That might take the curse off the theory *if* the hypothesis were necessary for explanatory purposes. But it is not. The origin of the state can be satisfactorily explained without any recourse to such fictions as the social contract and the state of nature. Therein lies the philosophical mistake that needs correction.

### 3

The correction of the error turns on recognizing that the distinction between a natural and a conventional origin for the state or civil society is not a flat disjunction—an "either-or-but-not-both."

*If* a form of association is natural *only* in the sense in which insect societies are genetically determined by instinctive endowments that are peculiar to a particular species, and *if* a form of association is conventional *only* in the sense in which private corporations or business and professional associations originate as a result of voluntary agreement on the part of the associating persons, *then* perforce it follows that no form of association can be *both* natural and conventional. It must be either the one or the other.

The modern exponents of the social contract theory knew that, historically, men did not always live in civil societies and states. They also knew that when civil societies or states did come into existence they were not all structured or pat-

terned in the same way. Hence they could not regard the state as natural in that sense of "natural" which signifies the result of instinctive endowment. As they saw it, the only alternative was to regard the state as purely conventional, not natural in any sense at all.

The root of the error here lies in not recognizing two different senses of the word "natural," in one of which an association cannot be both natural and conventional, and in the other of which it can be both.

This other sense of the word "natural" was recognized in antiquity. A political philosopher, such as Aristotle, found no difficulty in describing the state or political community as *both* natural and conventional.

Among the three major exponents of the social contract theory in modern times, Rousseau alone reveals that he, too, recognized the sense in which the state may be natural as well as conventional. Unfortunately, the recognition was subliminal and never came to the surface explicitly. Rousseau never abandoned the fictions of a state of nature and a social contract to explain the origin of civil society.

The subliminal recognition referred to above occurred as follows in Rousseau. In Book I, Chapter 2, of *The Social Contract* Rousseau wrote:

The most ancient of all societies, and the *only one that is natural* [italics added], is the family: and even so the children remain attached to the father *only so long as they need him for their preservation* [italics added]. As soon as this need ceases, the natural bond is dissolved.

The family is thus seen to be natural because there is a natural need for it, not because human beings are geneti-

cally determined by instinct to set up relatively permanent domestic groups.

That these domestic societies are natural by need, not natural by instinct, also becomes apparent from the fact that human families are organized in a multitude of different ways. They would not be if they were instinctively determined instead of being formed voluntarily and by free choices. The human family is thus both natural and conventional.

In Book I, Chapter 6, entitled "The Social Compact," Rousseau's opening paragraph reads as follows:

> I suppose men to have reached the point at which obstacles in the way of their preservation in the state of nature show their power of resistance to be greater than the resources at the disposal of each individual for his maintenance in that state. That primitive condition can then subsist no longer; and the human race would perish unless it changed its manner of existence.

Why, then, did human beings depart from the mythical or hypothetical state of nature (in which they never did exist, because they always lived in families at least)? They were not driven to do so by innate instinct. They were driven by a natural need, just as they were driven to live in families by a natural need. Civil society is just as natural as the family, and natural in the same sense.

But is the natural need the same? No, for the small domestic society, or isolated family, and the enlarged society that consists of consanguineous families associated in tribes and villages, suffice for the mere preservation of human life. The labor of the members of a family, or the population of a tribe, provides the daily means of subsistence, or a little

more than that, which can be stored for times of deprivation. The state or civil society does not come into existence for such purposes nor to satisfy the need for the preservation of the species.

Rousseau tacitly admits this when, in the closing chapter of the first book, he calls attention to the difference between primitive and civilized life ("civilized" in the sense of being lived in civil society or a political community). The state or civil society came into existence to satisfy man's natural need for the conditions requisite for achieving a morally good human life—*not just to live, but to live well.*

The so-called "state of nature" being nonexistent and the naturalness of civil society being founded upon a natural need, not upon innate instincts, why does anyone still persist in the myth that men came together out of a state of nature to enter into a social contract with one another to institute civil society or the state? Is no other explanation of the origin of the state available?

Yes, there is one that can appeal to the facts of recorded history. The earliest political communities emerged out of large tribal organizations which, for one reason or another, associated with one another to form a still larger society—that of associated tribes or villages. The kind of rule or government that prevailed in the tribes, an absolute rule by the elders, carried over into the larger societies they formed by coming together. Instead of tribal chieftains, they now had kings, ruling absolutely or despotically, as did the great kings of Persia or the pharaohs of Egypt.

A little later, the absolute or despotic rule of kings was replaced by the adoption of constitutions in the city-states of Greece. Solon gave the Athenians a constitution which, adopted by them voluntarily, established the Athenian re-

public. So, too, Lycurgus gave the Spartans a constitution out of which, again by voluntary adoption, the Spartan republic came into existence.

Aware of this history, Aristotle, after stressing the naturalness of the state because of the natural need it satisfied, wrote that "he who first founded the state was the greatest of benefactors." He had Solon and Lycurgus in mind as founders of the state because, in his view, absolute or despotic rule, carried over from the rule of tribal chieftains, was incompatible with a state—a civil society or political community.

If human beings are by nature not just social but also political, then they have a natural inclination and need to participate in government. That is possible only when they become citizens of a republic and live under constitutional government. They then have political liberty, which means being governed with one's own consent and having a voice in one's own government.

The voluntary adoption of a constitution that creates a republic, with the citizens as the ruling class and the administrators of government always citizens holding public office with constitutionally limited authority and power, is a much better, historically more accurate, account of the origin of the state than Rousseau's theory of the social contract.

Rousseau, no less than Aristotle, regarded a republic, or a civil society under constitutional government, as the only legitimate form of civil government. Without it, there cannot be a truly political community. The other forms under absolute or despotic rule are anomalous, neither strictly tribal organizations nor truly political communities.

4

Two other errors should be mentioned briefly. One is made by Rousseau when he says that, after individuals have agreed to form a civil society under the terms of the social contract, each person "while uniting himself with all, may still obey himself alone and remain as free as before."

Living under government, even the most perfectly devised constitutional government, makes it impossible for the individual to obey himself alone. He does not "remain as free as before," by which Rousseau means as free as he was in a state of nature before he entered into the social contract. His freedom in the mythical state of nature was complete autonomy. He was a law unto himself.

He had to abandon that complete autonomy, according to Rousseau, when, by the social contract or any other means, he became a member of civil society. What then replaced the unlimited freedom of complete autonomy was the limited freedom of civil liberty—freedom under government, not freedom from government.

The mention of complete autonomy as incompatible with living in civil society under government brings us to one other characteristically modern error about human society. It is an error that cannot be found in ancient or mediaeval times. It emerges in the nineteenth century with such philosophical anarchists as Kropotkin, Bakunin, Marx, and Lenin.

The error consists in thinking that it is possible for men to live together peacefully and harmoniously in society without government and without just laws made effective by the exercise of coercive force. More than merely possible, that is the ideal held up by Kropotkin and Bakunin—

the elimination of the state and government as irremediably evil.

Differing from Bakunin, who advocated the overthrow of the state by direct action, Marx and Lenin can be described as Fabian anarchists. In their view, the ultimate ideal of communism will be realized after the dictatorship of the proletariat, which is the penultimate approach to the ideal of communism, liquidates itself. Then the oppressive state, with the coercive force of its government and laws, will gradually wither away.

By either route the utopia envisaged is peaceful anarchy, than which nothing could be more impossible, given human nature as it is. The Marxist view is that when external conditions, especially the conditions under which wealth is produced and distributed, are radically altered, so, too, will be the nature of man. A new man will emerge, one capable of living peacefully and harmoniously with his fellows and without regulation by government or restraint by coercively enforced laws.

The notion of "the new man" is as much a myth as the notions of "a state of nature" and of "the social contract." The utopian fantasy of peaceful anarchy is as impracticable and unrealizable as any utopia ever dreamed up.*

*In an earlier book of mine, *The Angels and Us* (1982), Chapter 11, entitled "Angelistic Politics," briefly gives all the reasons why peaceful anarchy is a utopian fantasy as well as an angelistic fallacy.

# CHAPTER 10
# Human Existence

### 1

WHAT DO PEOPLE HAVE in mind when they inquire about the existence of anything?

First of all, they are asking about whether the thing in question has reality. Does it exist in the real world quite independent of our minds and whatever we may think or know, or is it only an object that exists for us when we exercise our powers of perception and thought?

A second question they may have in mind concerns the manner of existence. Does it exist in and by itself, not as a part or aspect of anything else, or is it merely the latter? If it exists alongside other things which, taken all together as an organized aggregate, constitute the whole of reality, then, of course, it exists as a part, and not entirely in and by itself. But if, when one of these other things ceases to exist, it still continues in existence, then it is not a part of

that thing in the sense in which the leg of a table would cease to exist if the table did.

What I have just said about the leg of a table can also be said about its color, its shape, its weight, and so on. These are attributes or characteristics of the table. As such, they do not exist in and by themselves; they exist in the table, and continue to exist only as long as the table does.

In ancient philosophy, the words "substance" and "accident" were used to make this distinction between that which existed in itself and that which existed in another. These terms no longer have currency and may be misleading. I am, therefore, going to substitute for them the more familiar words "thing" and "attribute" for what was once spoken of as having substantial and accidental existence.

Still another question concerns the duration or durability of existence. As compared with a thing, or even with its attributes, events are existences of short duration. A lightning flash, for example, we regard as an instantaneous event; a long peal of thunder, as an event of short duration, having a beginning, middle, and end within a brief span of time. We would not, therefore, refer to it as a thing. In contrast, a house that has been standing for a century or more, undergoing change during that time, is not an event but a thing.

In the world of material, physical phenomena, things are the only existences that are the subjects of change. Events do not change. The attributes of a thing do not change. The greenness of an apple that has not yet ripened does not become red when the ripening occurs. On the contrary, it is the apple that has altered in quality, changing from green to red. It is the apple that changes in place when it is moved from here to there. And it is the human baby

that changes in size and weight, and in many other respects, when it grows, not the attributes or characteristics that are replaced by other attributes or characteristics when these changes take place with growth.

The mutable existence of things involves another point of great importance. For a thing to change in whatever respect, it itself must remain that one and the same thing throughout the process. If it did not remain the same thing, how could we possibly speak of *it* as changing?

In short, that which is the subject of change must have an enduring identifiable identity. It must also have a persistent unity. If the thing is a whole that has component parts it is, of course, divisible; but while it remains a single subject of change, it must remain undivided. When it is divided, it ceases to be that one individual thing.

How, then, does a human being exist? Our common sense of the matter, based upon our common experience, is that human beings exist as individual things, having many attributes with respect to which they change while they remain one and the same enduring thing that is subject to all these changes.

What has just been said may seem simple and obvious, perhaps hardly worth saying, but it is a matter of no slight importance. Without the kind of identifiable identity that belongs to the individual thing as a subject of change, human beings, having obviously mutable existence, could not be held morally responsible for their acts.

Our own sense of our personal identity is that, from moment to moment, sleeping or waking, we are one and the same individual, the same whole of parts, the same bearer of many attributes. We do not cease to be that one individual thing, even if, with surgical amputation, we lose a part

of our body; or, in the course of aging, we undergo radical changes in our physical characteristics, our personal attributes, our temperamental traits.

We regard other human beings in the same light in which we view ourselves. They, too, have an identifiable identity, an enduring oneness and sameness while they undergo change. We do not experience their identity as we experience our own, but we have no doubt that they possess it in the same way that we do, and that through it they have the same moral responsibility for their acts that we have for ours.

Our common sense of the matter goes further than that. All the physical objects in the world of our daily perceptual experience—the chairs and tables, the houses and automobiles, the pet animals, the trees and plants in the garden, the stones and statues—all these are individual things, enduring identities that are subject to change. And we think of them as possessing the various sensible qualities—the colors, textures, odors, and so on—that we experience them as having.

2

This common-sense picture of the world in which we live would appear to be shattered by what we are told by the physical scientists of our own day.

I will never forget my shock when, more than fifty years ago, I read Sir Arthur Eddington's Gifford Lectures, *The Nature of the Physical World*. In his opening remarks, Sir Arthur told his audience that the table in front of which he was standing, the table which seemed so solid to them that they would bruise their fists if they tried to punch through it, was in reality an area of largely empty space in

which tiny invisible bodies were moving about at great speeds, interacting with one another in a variety of ways, and making the table appear to us to be solid, of a certain size, shape, and weight, and having certain other sensible qualities, such as its color, its smoothness, and so on.

*Appearance and reality!* As Sir Arthur spoke, there seemed to be no doubt in his mind which was which. The table the lecturer and his audience perceived through their eyes and could touch with their hands might appear to them to be an individual thing that had an enduring identifiable identity which could undergo change while remaining one and the same thing. That was the appearance, an appearance that might even be called illusory in comparison to the invisible and untouchable reality of the atomic particles in motion that filled the space occupied by the visible table, a space largely empty even though impenetrable by us.

My initial shock increased when I passed from thinking about the table to thinking about myself and other human beings. We were not different from the table. We, too, were individual physical things. We might appear to ourselves and to each other to be as solid as the table, perhaps somewhat softer to the touch, but just as impenetrable to a probing finger. But, in reality, the space our apparently solid bodies occupied was just as empty as that of the table. Whatever attributes or characteristics our bodies appear to have as we perceive them through our senses, they have as a result of the motions and interactions of particles that themselves had none of these sensible characteristics.

(According to this view, the imperceptible particles that compose all the objects of our ordinary perceptual experi-

ence possess only quantitative properties, no sensible qualities at all. The latter, it is maintained, exist only in our consciousness of the objects we perceive, not in the objects themselves. They have no status in reality. Thus arises the riddle about what came to be called "secondary qualities," a puzzlement that always accompanies the reductionist fallacy to which atomists are prone.)

What becomes of my personal identity, or yours, and with it moral responsibility for our actions, if each of us ceases to be one individual thing, but becomes instead a congeries of physical particles that do not remain the same particles during the span of our lifetime?

To face the problem that here is raised, let us eliminate at once an easy way out of the difficulty. That easy way out is to regard both pictures—the one we have as a matter of common sense and common experience and the one we are given by atomic physicists—as convenient and useful fictions. The first of these serves all the practical exigencies of our daily lives. The second, applied through technological innovations, gives us extraordinary mastery and control over the physical world in which we live.

Approached this way, there is no conflict between the two views of the world in which we live and of ourselves as living organisms existing in it. We need not ask which is the reality and which is the mere appearance or illusion.

Before the middle of the last century, the theory of the atomists was regarded as positing a useful scientific fiction, and so it posed no challenge to the reality of the common-sense view that a sound philosophy endorsed. Until then, beginning with Democritus in the ancient world and coming down to Newton and Dalton in the modern world, the

atom was conceived as the absolutely indivisible unit of matter. In the words of Lucretius, it was a unit of "solid singleness," with no void within it, as there must be a void in any composite and, therefore, divisible body having atoms as its component parts.

We know that in the late nineteenth century, and in our own day, all this has been radically changed. There is no longer any doubt about the real existence of atoms, which are now known to be divisible and to be as much filled microscopically with void or empty space as the solar system is filled macroscopically. In that empty space move the elementary particles that have now been discovered by the most ingenious detecting devices, the real existence of which is supposedly verified by inferences from the observed phenomena, phenomena that cannot be explained except by positing the real existence of these unobservable particles.

Let me make sure that the last point is fully clear. The elementary particles, which are the moving components of the divisible atom, are intrinsically imperceptible to our senses. As a contemporary writer puts it, they are essentially unpicturable—"unpicturable-in-principle." They and the atoms they constitute do not have any of the sensible qualities possessed by the perceptible physical things of common experience. Nor do the elementary particles even have the quantitative properties possessed by atoms and molecules, such as size, weight, shape, or configuration.

Werner Heisenberg's statement of the matter confirms how radical, indeed, is the unpicturability of the elementary particles. He writes as follows:

The indivisible elementary particle of modern physics possesses the quality of taking up space in no higher measure than other

properties, say color and strength of material. [They] are no longer material bodies in the proper sense of the word.★

Heisenberg goes on to say that they are units of matter only in the sense in which mass and energy are interchangeable. This fundamental stuff, according to him, "is capable of existence in different forms," but "always appears in definite quanta."† These quanta of mass/energy cannot even be exclusively described as particles, for they are as much waves or wave packets.

Speaking of atoms and molecules, are we not called upon to say of them what we seem to be called upon to say of ourselves and the other perceptible things of common experience? They, too, are divisible wholes made up of moving and changing components. What about their reality as compared with that of the elementary particles that constitute them? If we could perceive with our naked eyes an atom or a molecule, would we not be compelled to say that it only appeared to be what it was perceived as—a solid, indivisible body—but that in reality what we perceived was only an illusion?

What we are confronted with here is the fallacy of reductionism, a mistake that has become most prevalent in our own day, not only among scientists but also among contemporary philosophers. It consists in regarding the ultimate constituents of the physical world as more real than the composite bodies these elementary components constitute. Reductionism may go even further and declare these ultimate constituents to be the only reality, relegating everything else to the status of mere appearance or illusion.

★ *Philosophic Problems of Nuclear Science*, pp. 55-56.
†*Ibid.*, p. 103.

### 3

How is this fallacy of reductionism, this philosophical mistake, to be corrected, as it must be if our common-sense view of things and if a philosophy of nature that accords with it is to be validated?

Before I attempt to suggest a solution, let me make sure that the conflict between the scientific and the common-sense view is clear. The chair on which I am now sitting fills a certain area of space. To say, on the one hand, that that space envelope is filled with the single, solid body that we experience as the perceived chair contradicts saying, on the other hand, that that space envelope is largely a void filled by moving and interacting imperceptible particles.

The conflict or contradiction here is not simply between filled and empty space. It involves a contradiction between the one and the many. The chair of our common experience, the reality of which a philosophy based on common sense defends, is not only a solid body, but even more fundamentally it is a single being. The chair of physical theory consists of an irreducible multiplicity of discrete units, each having its own individual existence.

If the unitary being which is the solid chair, with all its sensible qualities, is dismissed as an illusion foisted on us by our sense-experience, then no conflict remains. Or if the physicist's atoms, elementary particles, wave packets, or quanta of mass and quanta of energy are merely theoretical entities to which no real existence is attributed (that is, if they are merely mathematical forms which have no physical reality), then their being posited for theoretical purposes as useful fictions does not challenge the view that what really exists out there is the solid chair of our experience.

If, however, real existence *of the same kind* is attributed to the entities described by the common-sense view and by the scientific view, then we cannot avoid a conflict that must be resolved.

A clue or hint that leads to the solution is contained in the italicized words in the preceding statement: "of the same kind." Both the solid chair and the imperceptible particles have real existence, but their reality is not of the same kind, not of the same order or degree. By virtue of that fact, the conflict can be resolved. The contradiction is then seen to be only apparent.

The problem would be insoluble if the two assertions to be reconciled stood in relation to one another in the same way that the statement that Jones is sitting in a particular chair at a particular time stands to the statement that Smith is sitting in the same chair at the same time, and is not sitting on top of Jones or on the arm of the chair, but exactly where Jones is sitting. The statements about Jones and Smith cannot both be true. They cannot be reconciled.

The assertion about the nuclear particles as the imperceptible constituents of the chair and the assertion about the perceptible solid chair as an individual thing, both occupying the same space, can be reconciled on condition that we recognize different grades or degrees of reality.

Werner Heisenberg used the term *potentia*—potentialities for being—to describe the very low, perhaps even the least, degree of reality that can be possessed by elementary particles. He wrote:

In the experiments about atomic events we have to do with things and facts, with phenomena that are just as real as any phenomena in daily life. But the atoms or the elementary particles themselves are

*not as real; they form a world of potentialities or possibilities rather than one of things or facts.*\*

Heisenberg, in saying that the elementary particles are *not as real* as the perceptible individual things of daily life, does not deny that they still have some reality.

The merely possible, that which has no actual existence at all, has no reality. That which has some potentiality for existence and tends toward existence has some, perhaps the least, degree of reality. It is barely more than merely possible.

Let me now summarize the solution of the problem, which corrects the philosophical mistake that arises from the fallacy of reductionism. It involves two steps.

(1) The reality of the elementary particles of nuclear physics cannot be reconciled with the reality of the chair as an individual sensible substance if both the particles and the chair are asserted to have the same mode of existence or grade of being. The same thing can also be said about the nuclear particles and the atoms of which they are component parts. The particles are less real than the atoms; that is, they have less actuality. This, I take it, is the meaning of Heisenberg's statement that the particles are in a state of *potentia*—"possibilities for being or tendencies for being."

(2) The mode of being of the material constituents of a physical body cannot be the same when those constituents exist in isolation and when they enter into the constitution of an actual body. Thus, when the chair exists actually as one body, the multitude of atoms and elementary particles which constitute it exist only virtually. Since their existence is only virtual, so is their multiplicity; and their vir-

\**Physics and Philosophy*, p. 186 (italics added).

tual multiplicity is not incompatible with the actual unity of the chair. Again, the same thing can also be said about a single atom and the nuclear particles which constitute it; or about a single molecule and the various atoms which constitute it. When an atom or a molecule actually exists as a unit of matter, its material constituents have only virtual existence and, consequently, their multiplicity is also only virtual.

What exists virtually has more reality than the merely potential and less than the fully actual. The virtually existing components of any composite whole become fully actual only when that composite decomposes or breaks up into its constituent parts.

The virtual existence and multiplicity of the material constituents do not abrogate their capacity for actual existence and actual multiplicity. If the unitary chair—or a single atom—were exploded into its ultimate material constituents, the elementary particles would assume the mode of actual existence which isolated particles have in a cyclotron; their virtual multiplicity would be transformed into an actual multitude.

The critical point here is that the mode of existence in which the particles are discrete units and have actual multiplicity cannot be the same as the mode of existence that they have when they are material constituents of the individual chair in actual existence.

If we assign the same mode of existence to the particles in a cyclotron and to the particles that enter into the constitution of an actual chair, the conflict between nuclear physics and the philosophical doctrine that affirms the reality of the material objects of common experience ceases to be merely an apparent conflict. It is a real conflict, and an ir-

resolvable one, because the conflicting theories are irreconcilable. But if they are assigned different modes of existence, the theories that appear to be in conflict can be reconciled.

Not only is the conflict between the view of the physical world advanced by physical science and the view held by common sense reconciled. We also reach the conclusion that the perceptible individual things of common experience have a higher degree of actual reality. This applies also to the sensible qualities—the so-called "secondary qualities"—that we experience these things as having. They are not merely figments of our consciousness with no status at all in the real world that is independent of our senses and our minds.

With this conclusion reached, the challenge to the reality of human existence and to the identifiable identity of the individual person is removed. There can be no question about the moral responsibility that each of us bears for his or her actions.

# EPILOGUE
# Modern Science and Ancient Wisdom

1

THE OUTSTANDING ACHIEVEMENT and intellectual glory of modern times has been empirical science and the mathematics that it has put to such good use. The progress it has made in the last three centuries, together with the technological advances that have resulted therefrom, are breathtaking.

The equally great achievement and intellectual glory of Greek antiquity and of the Middle Ages was philosophy. We have inherited from those epochs a fund of accumulated wisdom. That, too, is breathtaking, especially when one considers how little philosophical progress has been made in modern times.

This is not to say that no advances in philosophical thought have occurred in the last three hundred years. They are mainly in logic, in the philosophy of science, and in

political theory, not in metaphysics, in the philosophy of nature, or in the philosophy of mind, and least of all in moral philosophy. Nor is it true to say that, in Greek antiquity and in the later Middle Ages, from the fourteenth century on, science did not prosper at all. On the contrary, the foundations were laid in mathematics, in mathematical physics, in biology, and in medicine.

It is in metaphysics, the philosophy of nature, the philosophy of mind, and moral philosophy that the ancients and their mediaeval successors did more than lay the foundations for the sound understanding and the modicum of wisdom we possess. They did not make the philosophical mistakes that have been the ruination of modern thought. On the contrary, they had the insights and made the indispensable distinctions that provide us with the means for correcting these mistakes.

At its best, investigative science gives us knowledge of reality. As I have argued earlier in this book, philosophy is, at the very least, also knowledge of reality, not mere opinion. Much better than that, it is knowledge illuminated by understanding. At its best, it approaches wisdom, both speculative and practical.

Precisely because science is investigative and philosophy is not, one should not be surprised by the remarkable progress in science and by the equally remarkable lack of it in philosophy. Precisely because philosophy is based upon the common experience of mankind and is a refinement and elaboration of the common-sense knowledge and understanding that derives from reflection on that common experience, philosophy came to maturity early and developed beyond that point only slightly and slowly.

Scientific knowledge changes, grows, improves, ex-

pands, as a result of refinements in and accretions to the special experience—the observational data—on which science as an investigative mode of inquiry must rely. Philosophical knowledge is not subject to the same conditions of change or growth. Common experience, or more precisely, the general lineaments or common core of that experience, which suffices for the philosopher, remains relatively constant over the ages.

Descartes and Hobbes in the seventeenth century, Locke, Hume, and Kant in the eighteenth century, and Alfred North Whitehead and Bertrand Russell in the twentieth century enjoy no greater advantages in this respect than Plato and Aristotle in antiquity or than Thomas Aquinas, Duns Scotus, and Roger Bacon in the Middle Ages.

## 2

How might modern thinkers have avoided the philosophical mistakes that have been so disastrous in their consequences? In earlier chapters I have suggested the answer. Finding a prior philosopher's conclusions untenable, the thing to do is to go back to his starting point and see if he has made a little error in the beginning.

A striking example of the failure to follow this rule is to be found in Kant's response to Hume. Hume's skeptical conclusions and his phenomenalism were unacceptable to Kant, even though they awoke him from his own dogmatic slumbers. But instead of looking for little errors in the beginning that were made by Hume and then dismissing them as the cause of the Humean conclusions that he found unacceptable, Kant thought it necessary to construct a vast piece of philosophical machinery designed to produce conclusions of an opposite tenor.

The intricacy of the apparatus and the ingenuity of the design cannot help but evoke admiration, even from those who are suspicious of the sanity of the whole enterprise and who find it necessary to reject Kant's conclusions as well as Hume's. Though they are opposite in tenor, they do not help us to get at the truth, which can only be found by correcting Hume's little errors in the beginning, and the little errors made by Locke and Descartes before that. To do that one must be in the possession of insights and distinctions with which these modern thinkers were unacquainted. Why they were, I will try to explain presently.

What I have just said about Kant in relation to Hume applies also to the whole tradition of British empirical philosophy from Hobbes, Locke, and Hume on. All of the philosophical puzzlements, paradoxes, and pseudo-problems that linguistic and analytical philosophy and therapeutic positivism in our own century have tried to eliminate would never have arisen in the first place if the little errors in the beginning made by Locke and Hume had been explicitly rejected instead of going unnoticed.

How did those little errors in the beginning arise in the first place? One answer is that something which needed to be known or understood had not yet been discovered or learned. Such mistakes are excusable, however regrettable they may be.

The second answer is that the errors are made as a result of culpable ignorance—ignorance of an essential point, an indispensable insight or distinction, that has already been discovered and expounded.

It is mainly in the second way that modern philosophers have made their little errors in the beginning. They are ugly monuments to the failures of education—failures due, on

the one hand, to corruptions in the tradition of learning and, on the other hand, to an antagonistic attitude toward or even contempt for the past, for the achievements of those who have come before.

### 3

Ten years ago, in 1974–1975, I wrote my autobiography, an intellectual biography entitled *Philosopher at Large*. As I now reread its concluding chapter, I can see the substance of this book emerging from what I wrote there.

I frankly confessed my commitment to Aristotle's philosophical wisdom, both speculative and practical, and to that of his great disciple Thomas Aquinas. The essential insights and the indispensable distinctions needed to correct the philosophical mistakes made in modern times are to be found in their thought.

Some things said in the concluding chapter of that book bear repetition here in the concluding chapter of this book. Since I cannot improve upon what I wrote ten years ago, I shall excerpt and paraphrase what I said then.

In the eyes of my contemporaries the label "Aristotelian" has dyslogistic connotations. It has had such connotations since the beginning of modern times. To call a man an Aristotelian carries with it highly derogatory implications. It suggests that his is a closed mind, in such slavish subjection to the thought of one philosopher as to be impervious to the insights or arguments of others.

However, it is certainly possible to be an Aristotelian— or the devoted disciple of some other philosopher—without also being a blind and slavish adherent of his views, declaring with misplaced piety that he is right in everything he says, never in error, or that he has cornered the

market on truth and is in no respect deficient or defective.

Such a declaration would be so preposterous that only a fool would affirm it. Foolish Aristotelians there must have been among the decadent scholastics who taught philosophy in the universities of the sixteenth and seventeenth centuries. They probably account for the vehemence of the reaction against Aristotle, as well as the flagrant misapprehension or ignorance of his thought, that is to be found in Thomas Hobbes and Francis Bacon, in Descartes, Spinoza, and Leibniz.

The folly is not the peculiar affliction of Aristotelians. Cases of it can certainly be found, in the last century, among those who gladly called themselves Kantians or Hegelians; and in our own day, among those who take pride in being disciples of John Dewey or Ludwig Wittgenstein. But if it is possible to be a follower of one of the modern thinkers without going to an extreme that is foolish, it is no less possible to be an Aristotelian who rejects Aristotle's error and deficiencies while embracing the truths he is able to teach.

Even granting that it is possible to be an Aristotelian without being doctrinaire about it, it remains the case that being an Aristotelian is somehow less respectable in recent centuries and in our time than being a Kantian or a Hegelian, an existentialist, a utilitarian, a pragmatist, or some other "ist" or "ian." I know, for example, that many of my contemporaries were outraged by my statement that Aristotle's *Ethics* is a unique book in the Western tradition of moral philosophy, the only ethics that is sound, practical, and undogmatic.

If a similar statement were made by a disciple of Kant or John Stuart Mill in a book that expounded and de-

fended the Kantian or utilitarian position in moral philosophy, it would be received without raised eyebrows or shaking heads. For example, in this century it has been said again and again, and gone unchallenged, that Bertrand Russell's theory of descriptions has been crucially pivotal in the philosophy of language; but it simply will not do for me to make exactly the same statement about the Aristotelian and Thomistic theory of signs (adding that it puts Russell's theory of descriptions into better perspective than the current view of it does).

Why is this so? My only answer is that it must be believed that, because Aristotle and Aquinas did their thinking so long ago, they cannot reasonably be supposed to have been right in matters about which those who came later were wrong. Much must have happened in the realm of philosophical thought during the last three or four hundred years that requires an open-minded person to abandon their teachings for something more recent and, therefore, supposedly better.

My response to that view is negative. I have found faults in the writings of Aristotle and Aquinas, but it has not been my reading of modern philosophical works that has called my attention to these faults, nor helped me to correct them. On the contrary, it has been my understanding of the underlying principles and the formative insights that govern the thought of Aristotle and Aquinas that has provided the basis for amending or amplifying their views where they are fallacious or defective.

I must say once more that in philosophy, both speculative and practical, few if any advances have been made in modern times. On the contrary, much has been lost as the result of errors that might have been avoided if ancient

truths had been preserved in the modern period instead of being ignored.

Modern philosophy, as I see it, got off to a very bad start—with Hobbes and Locke in England, and with Descartes, Spinoza, and Leibniz on the Continent. Each of these thinkers acted as if he had no predecessors worth consulting, as if he were starting with a clean slate to construct for the first time the whole of philosophical knowledge.

We cannot find in their writings the slightest evidence of their sharing Aristotle's insight that no man by himself is able to attain the truth adequately, although collectively men do not fail to amass a considerable amount; nor do they ever manifest the slightest trace of a willingness to call into council the views of their predecessors in order to profit from whatever is sound in their thought and to avoid their errors. On the contrary, without anything like a careful, critical examination of the views of their predecessors, these modern thinkers issue blanket repudiations of the past as a repository of errors. The discovery of philosophical truth begins with themselves.

Proceeding, therefore, in ignorance or misunderstanding of truths that could have been found in the funded tradition of almost two thousand years of Western thought, these modern philosophers made crucial mistakes in their points of departure and in their initial postulates. The commission of these errors can be explained in part by antagonism toward the past, and even contempt for it.

The explanation of the antagonism lies in the character of the teachers under whom these modern philosophers studied in their youth. These teachers did not pass on the philosophical tradition as a living thing by recourse to the writings of the great philosophers of the past. They did not

read and comment on the works of Aristotle, for example, as the great teachers of the thirteenth century did.

Instead, the decadent scholastics who occupied teaching posts in the universities of the sixteenth and seventeenth centuries fossilized the tradition by presenting it in a deadly, dogmatic fashion, using a jargon that concealed rather than conveyed the insights it contained. Their lectures must have been as wooden and uninspiring as most textbooks or manuals are; their examinations must have called for a verbal parroting of the letter of ancient doctrines rather than for an understanding of their spirit.

It is no wonder that early modern thinkers, thus mistaught, recoiled. Their repugnance, though certainly explicable, may not be wholly pardonable, for they could have repaired the damage by turning to the texts of Aristotle or Aquinas in their mature years and by reading them perceptively and critically.

That they did not do this can be ascertained from an examination of their major works and from their intellectual biographies. When they reject certain points of doctrine inherited from the past, it is perfectly clear that they do not properly understand them; in addition, they make mistakes that arise from ignorance of distinctions and insights highly relevant to problems they attempt to solve.

With very few exceptions, such misunderstanding and ignorance of philosophical achievements made prior to the sixteenth century have been the besetting sin of modern thought. Its effects are not confined to philosophers of the seventeenth and eighteenth centuries. They are evident in the work of nineteenth-century philosophers and in the writings of our day. We can find them, for example, in the works of Ludwig Wittgenstein, who, for all his native bril-

liance and philosophical fervor, stumbles in the dark in dealing with problems on which his premodern predecessors, unknown to him, have thrown great light.

Modern philosophy has never recovered from its false starts. Like men floundering in quicksand who compound their difficulties by struggling to extricate themselves, Kant and his successors have multiplied the difficulties and perplexities of modern philosophy by the very strenuousness—and even ingenuity—of their efforts to extricate themselves from the muddle left in their path by Descartes, Locke, and Hume.

To make a fresh start, it is only necessary to open the great philosophical books of the past (especially those written by Aristotle and in his tradition) and to read them with the effort of understanding that they deserve. The recovery of basic truths, long hidden from view, would eradicate errors that have had such disastrous consequences in modern times.

# Flat Broke with Children